D1268307

Divorce Demystified is a must-read for anyone contemplating or going through a divorce. I highly recommend it.

EDWARD SOSNICK
Former Family Court Judge (Retired)

Divorce Demystified is comprehensive, well-written, and covers a lot of important territory in a readable and interesting manner, both legally and psychologically.

DR. LARRY FRIEDBERG
Forensic Psychologist, Marriage and Family Therapist

Divorce Demystified is the best and most up-to-date book that I have read on the subject. It explains every step of your divorce from beginning to end in an interesting manner that is easy to understand.

STEVE PECK
Founder and Host of *DivorceSourceRadio.com*

TO PAUL

ALL THE BEST!

DIVORCE
demystified

HENRY S. GORNBEIN, ESQ.

MOMENTUM BOOKS L.L.C.
ROYAL OAK, MI

Copyright © 2014 by Henry S. Gornbein.

All rights reserved.
No part of this book may be used or reproduced in any manner whatsoever without prior
written permission of the publisher.

Printed and bound in the U.S.A.
Published by Momentum Books, L.L.C., a subsidiary of Hour Media, L.L.C.
117 West Third Street
Royal Oak, Michigan 48067
www.momentumbooks.com

ISBN-13: 978-1-938018-05-3
LCCN: 2014955448

Dedicated to my lovely wife Debra, in appreciation
for her patience and understanding.

CONTENTS

INTRODUCTION

Divorce is one of the most traumatic events a human can experience. It not only affects the couple involved, but can also be devastating for children, extended family, and friends.

Yet, divorce can be a good thing. It is a way out of a bad marriage and ideally, into a new, happier, more fulfilling life for all of the parties involved.

With this book, I hope to help readers avoid some of the drama and trauma surrounding divorce. As an attorney specializing in divorce and other family law matters for more than 40 years, I have seen it all and know this: Arming yourself with knowledge, keeping a level head, putting your children first if you have them, and being smart about how you conduct yourself before, during, and after the divorce will help make this bad situation better.

Divorce is complicated, often messy. It used to be that the wife got the children, the husband shelled out support, and de-coupling required a few signatures.

Not anymore. From social media and two-income families to pet parents and same-sex marriage, nearly every aspect of divorce has changed.

This book provides the tools and insights you'll need to navigate the process. My goal is to remove some of the drama. Besides exploring legal, economic, and psychological issues, I focus on the random, routine, and often overlooked details — like Facebook posts and tweets — that can propel divorce proceedings into a roller-coaster ride gone mad.

My hope is that by reading this book, your journey through divorce will be much less threatening, far more tolerable, and always based on sound knowledge.

— *Henry S. Gornbein, Esq.*
January 2015

CHAPTER ONE

A Team Approach To Your Divorce

A psychologist told me many years ago that the divorce rate is about 50 percent. He then went on to say that of the remaining 50 percent who remain married, half of the couples are unhappy.

In my experience, many clients who come to me because they're in very bad marriages will decide to hang in there. Conversely, others who might be able to save their marriages opt for divorce. There is often no rhyme or reason behind why people decide to file for divorce or remain in a dysfunctional marriage.

But divorce exists for a reason, and that is to help people extricate themselves from bad marriages. It should be handled properly — if possible, delicately.

I don't believe in a cookie-cutter approach to divorce. Every divorce is as different as the needs and desires of the individuals involved.

Over the years I have developed and used a team approach to divorce. In football terminology, the attorney is like the quarterback who is overseeing the team, guiding you through the legal system with the help of other key players on the team.

TEAM MEMBERS

My office team includes other attorneys who specialize in family law as well as a paralegal who works closely with me to assist each client. There is always someone available to help our clients every step of the way.

Next on the team is a therapist — important for many reasons that are discussed in various parts of this book. With my client signing a release to waive confidentiality, I often communicate regularly with the therapist as the divorce progresses. This is very helpful to the client, the therapist, and myself.

For example, I can discuss legal issues with the therapist that may be frightening to the client. That arms the therapist with information to allay some of the fears and nervousness that so often accompany the divorce process. Conversely, if there is a particular issue troubling my client, the therapist may give me advice that can be useful as the client, therapist, and I strategize on how to deal with various issues — especially when there are children involved.

Another key team member is the mediator. I believe wholeheartedly in the mediation process, which can be win-win for everyone. I also believe early-stage mediation is effective for trying to deal with contentious issues sooner rather than later.

Other experts also become part of the team, depending on the circumstances. For example, many divorces involve homes and/or other real estate that need to be valued so an informed decision can be made on whether to keep or sell such assets. Here, a real estate appraiser can be critical, whether for residential or commercial real estate.

When a home is going to be sold, having an experienced Realtor can be important.

Many of my clients are involved in businesses that can range from restaurants and gas stations to professional practices. In these situations, it is important to have an accountant or other expert to appraise and put a value on the business or professional practice.

If there are allegations of an affair or other inappropriate behavior, it may prove necessary to bring in a private investigator.

In cases involving bankruptcy, there may be a need for a bankruptcy attorney.

When debt consolidation and other negotiations regarding financial issues are in the mix, a specialist in this realm can be helpful.

Many divorces involve wills and trusts and estate plans. An expert may be needed to ensure that there are agreements not only for the divorce, but also that your estate plan is updated now that you are no longer going to be married.

In many cases, there are issues involving the management and transfer of assets. In these situations, financial planners and money managers can be invaluable.

In divorces where there are pensions or other tax-deferred assets, Qualified Domestic Orders are used to transfer 401(k)s and other retirement assets, including pensions, from one party to another. Often, specialists in this area are utilized as well.

Tax attorneys and accountants may need to be consulted on questions relating to tax planning fand income tax.

And sometimes, a business will have to be reorganized, with stock transferred. Here, a corporate or business attorney can be helpful.

When there are child-related issues, I work with child psychologists and other experts. If custody is a factor, it may be necessary to have an independent psychological evaluation of all parties.

Additional circumstances may call for other experts including divorce financial planners and divorce coaches, for example.

Regardless, the team approach makes a lot of sense as you move forward from your marriage to a new chapter of life. The better the team, the smoother your transition will be from living in a bad marriage to enjoying a healthier, happier life after divorce.

Wrapping Up

In many divorces, you need more than just an attorney as part of your team. A divorce touches many aspects of your life and the key is to involve different experts, depending on your needs and those of your family.

Notes

Notes

CHAPTER TWO

Divorce: Not One Size Fits All

Remember your wedding? It was a beautiful occasion, right? As you made the commitment to join together as husband and wife, in sickness and in health, for better or for worse, until death do you part, you anticipated spending the rest of your lives together.

Unfortunately, those wedding day ideals do not always translate to reality.

When I was growing up, divorces were uncommon. When they did occur, they were noted in hushed terms. There was a lot of stigma attached to divorce.

Today, almost everyone is touched by divorce — via a family member or friend, or personally. Go into any elementary or high school classroom and a large number of the children will be from divorced or blended families.

Too many people expect too much of marriage and are willing to give too little to make it work. In this age of instant gratification, people often marry with the idea of changing the ways of their new spouse. In many cases, female clients tell me that they thought that their husbands could change. Maybe he drank too much, but promised to make modifications after the marriage. This rarely works. I've found that people are on their best behavior until the marriage when, too often, Dr. Jekyll becomes Mr. Hyde.

Divorce is nothing to be ashamed of. People change, they grow apart, their goals and desires evolve in different directions. If a couple is not on the same page, divorce can be a good thing.

However, divorce is not simple. It is not one size fits all and encompasses many aspects: legal, psychological, economic, and religious.

THE LEGAL DIVORCE

Legal divorce is the process by which you go through the legal system with the end result being a judge pronouncing the end of your marriage. You walk out of court with a legal document called a judgment of divorce, or divorce decree.

That is often just the beginning, rather than the end. Your once-happy marriage is now a document that maps out how you go forward with your life and those of your children.

It is not a happy time to begin with. With children, it's even more complicated; while you and your spouse may divorce, your lives remain entwined because you are parents together.

THE PSYCHOLOGICAL DIVORCE

Being divorced in your mind is just as important — if not more so — as the legal divorce.

Psychologists have said that the hardest, most life-altering event is losing a child. Next comes the death of a spouse in an intact marriage. Third is the end of a marriage through divorce – one of the most gut-wrenching and traumatic experiences of a lifetime. You can never underestimate the impact of divorce on you and your children.

That's why divorce should always be a last resort – not a first. I will reiterate this point throughout the chapters of this book.

Think of a 100-yard dash. It is quick and relatively painless unless you are in terrible physical shape.

Now think of a marathon. No matter what physical and emotional shape you are in, a marathon is grueling to say the least. That 26-plus miles will seem insurmountable.

Divorce is like the marathon. I tell my clients: You will hit a wall. There will be points in your divorce that you will feel you cannot continue.

But, I assure them, you will prevail. There is life after divorce.

In many years of specializing in divorce, I have learned that if two people have reached a point where they are psychologically divorced and ready to move forward, the legal process will be simple. They will handle the legal and economic aspects in a civil and expeditious manner. The economic and emotional costs will be minimal.

However, if one spouse is ready to move on and disengage psychologically and the other is not, whether due to anger, bitterness, or one or both spouses having emotional problems, expect some fireworks. The legal process will not be simple and until each spouse is ready to let go and move on, there will be problems. The result will be an extra-complicated, expensive, and difficult divorce – one that is more of an emotional and legal roller coaster for everyone involved. These are often cases where one spouse has had an affair, or where there may be problems with alcohol or abuse driving one spouse to say that enough is enough even though the other spouse wants to continue with what is a truly dysfunctional marriage.

The worst scenario creates nightmares for not only the litigants, but also for the attorneys and judges involved. I call this the never-ending divorce because even when the divorce is finalized in court, the battle has just begun over anything from support and alimony issues to child custody disputes. In extreme cases, such squabbles continue until the children turn 18 – many years after the divorce was finalized. Those in this situation spend thousands of dollars on legal fees and go through numerous attorneys because they don't get the result that they want. In trying to hurt a former spouse, someone you once loved, you will destroy your children. Never forget that children are the innocent victims of such continuing wars in and out of court.

Sadly, I have handled many of these never-ending war cases. They are often fueled by rage, mental instability, and bitterness that lingers year after year.

The parties go from attorney to attorney, and therapist to therapist, seeking vindication and justification that never come. They are tragic, to say the least.

For example, I once had a case where my client's husband burned down the marital home rather than divide it with his wife. He ended up in prison. In another situation, a client refused to leave his wife and children alone and ended up on a tether after criminal charges were pressed against him.

With this book, I hope to help you avoid unnecessary litigation and confrontation. Instead, let your focus be on handling your divorce in a humane and civil manner. Realize that divorce is a transition: from an unhappy marriage to the next phase in your life.

THE ECONOMIC DIVORCE

During tough economic times, many people are already financially strapped. When they go through a divorce, the economics can become almost impossible.

There is an economic divorce because you are dividing your assets. You will normally have half of what you had before you filed for a divorce. There are debts to divide. And there can be added obligations in the form of child support, spousal support or alimony, and medical bills.

It's not unusual for everyone to be unhappy at the end of a divorce because the numbers too often don't add up. Even when they do, the budget is never the same as an intact marriage. Two living apart cannot live as cheaply as two living together. Whether you have millions of dollars or very little, the economic results can be a challenge. For these reasons, an economic divorce goes hand in hand with the legal, psychological, and in many instances, religious divorce.

THE RELIGIOUS DIVORCE

Catholicism and similar faiths require an annulment before either spouse can remarry within the Roman Catholic Church. Obtaining an annulment means following procedures and meeting vigorous requirements set forth by the denomination.

Judaism requires obtaining a "Get," or religious divorce, before a remarriage can take place. This is especially true if one is Orthodox or conservative and can lead to litigation because the husband has to consent to the Get and there are a lot of negotiations that can occur over this issue. The Get is obtained through a panel of rabbis who perform a special ceremony that ends the marriage in accordance with Jewish rituals that go back thousands of years.

Muslims require that a religious divorce ceremony be performed under the dictates of Islam through a sheik before a woman can remarry within the faith. Here again, the husband is the one who has to grant the Islamic divorce. In cases where I have represented members of the Muslim faith in a divorce, I make sure that this issue is covered as part of the written settlement agreement to avoid serious problems after the divorce.

These issues are all important in the overall scheme of your divorce. In the chapters to come, I will be providing you with the tools to deal with all aspects of your divorce.

Wrapping Up

There are four aspects of divorce: the legal divorce, the psychological divorce, the economic divorce, and last but not least, the religious divorce. Simply put, divorce is complicated.

Notes

Notes

CHAPTER THREE

The Internet Effect

Today, a video in California can go viral in hours and cause riots and murders thousands of miles away. We wake up every morning with the "Play Of The Day" on ABC's *Good Morning America*. Emails, texts, Twitter, Facebook, LinkedIn, and various websites are touching every aspect of our lives.

People get divorced for many reasons. The big ones include infidelity, domestic violence, abusive behavior, alcohol and other addiction issues, pornography, failure to communicate, and growing apart, just to name a few. What do the Internet and social media have to do with this?

The Internet speeds up everything. With Twitter, YouTube, and Facebook, it is almost as if we are living our lives on steroids.

Think of the office affair. People would meet and develop a gradual relationship that could often lead to trouble and the end of a marriage. These relationships would develop over weeks and months.

Now with the click of a computer key, one can meet anyone, anywhere, online. Everything happens more rapidly; courtship is not gradual. The Internet and social media speed everything up.

Countless websites target people who want to cheat on their spouses. Many of my clients have met someone online through these websites. I have also had multiple cases where people meet strangers online and then have a sexual encounter. The Internet makes it easier to become involved in an extramarital relationship and walk away from a marriage. People do stupid things and the Internet makes it simpler. It also facilitates hiding behind a false persona to be someone who you may want to be — but are not.

And people have their demons. The Internet makes it much easier to partake in forbidden fruit, lie, and cheat. People are anonymous; you can be anyone you want behind that computer screen and it's easier to mask the truth when you are not looking someone in the eye, face to face. It can also be dangerous. People have been kidnapped and even murdered by strangers they have met and trusted online.

Yet, people meet and have affairs more and more often through online connections. I have had clients on social dating sites even before divorce papers have been filed. Everyone is in a hurry, and the Internet and all of its ramifications make everything instantaneous.

ADDICTION CENTRAL

The Internet also fuels addiction. Consider pornography. While it predates the Internet, it was not so easily accessible before, requiring a drive to an adult bookstore or movie theater. Now with a click of a few computer keys, it's all there for anyone, including your children, to see.

I have seen many clients become addicted to pornography online. With thousands of sites catering to every possible taste, both legal and illegal, it's easy to spend a lot of money — and time — looking at X-rated material on the Web. I just settled a divorce in which my client's husband spent thousands of dollars on credit cards for pornographic sites featuring women on video cameras. Sure, clients bring in phone records and credit card receipts showing the monetary damage. But what about the emotional fallout?

Alcohol is available everywhere, but many people obtain prescription and illegal drugs online. Instead of being limited to a small geographic area, the Internet puts the world at your fingertips and on your computer screen, for better and for worse. Push a key and temptation is everywhere.

Some of my previous clients became addicted to online shopping, spending thousands on often-frivolous purchases, putting their family's financial stability at risk and leading to divorce. In one recent case, my client's wife spent many thousands of dollars in a few months at Amazon, Pottery Barn, and several other sites. Without leaving the house, this woman ran up more than $60,000 in credit card debt in just a few months.

Addiction to computer games, especially with children, has also been a factor in some of the divorces I've handled. In one case, both the husband and wife were at wits end with their son, who had dropped out of high school because of an addiction to computer games.

I have also seen many cases where one spouse spending hours immersed in the Internet led to a breakdown of the marriage. These people will spend their days texting, emailing, and generally no longer communicating with their spouses and children. I can tell you endless stories of clients who come to me because a husband or wife returns from work only to disappear into the world of the Internet, whether for pornography, games, Facebook, gambling, or myriad other endless scenarios. In addition to the Internet, many people can't tear themselves away from texting, sexting, and doing everything possible to avoid communicating with their families as they are totally occupied with their cellphones and iPads.

One spouse losing hundreds of thousands of dollars gambling online has meant the end of many marriages. Again, the easy access of poker and other gambling sites is endless. Thousands of dollars can be lost by simply pressing a computer key.

Day trading can also cause problems. Some of my clients have spouses who spend every waking hour when not at work buying and selling stocks online. It is easy and can be dangerous, and have severe economic and emotional consequences.

Whatever the vice, the Internet provides easy access. When one of my clients found her husband watching child pornography online, she called the police and filed for divorce. In addition to the demise of the marriage, her husband ended up in jail.

Human frailties are magnified by the Internet, which is having a major impact on the types of and reasons for divorces. Every attorney — and therapist — I talk to feels the same way.

Wrapping Up

The Internet is playing an increasingly prominent role in the demise of marriages today. It has drastically changed the landscape of marriage and divorce, adding still another layer to the already complicated process divorcing couples find themselves dealing with — not only in relation to the breakup of a marriage, but also in creating more issues during the divorce process.

Notes

_____

_____

_____

_____

_____

_____

_____

_____

_____

_____

_____

_____

_____

_____

_____

_____

_____

_____

_____

_____

_____

_____

_____

_____

_____

CHAPTER FOUR

Navigating Social Media

1
2
3
4
5
6
7
8
9
10
11
12
13
14
15
16
17
18
19
20
21

I have been a lecturer for nationwide webinars designed specifically for attorneys and covering such issues as spying on spouses, electronic data evidence, and what's legal in the digital world when it comes to divorce. It's complicated, unfolding—and a seemingly ever-present factor in today's divorce proceedings in one way or another.

For example, I recently met with a woman who was going through a divorce. She had mistakenly received a text message intended for someone else. That led her to a photo of her husband on a gay dating site. After years of marriage, she had learned that her husband was gay.

I have seen numerous situations in which spouses learn about affairs through Facebook. People will put pictures on Facebook that show their children with an uncle (boyfriend), or some person of the opposite sex whom the spouse has never heard of. This can be important in a divorce where custody is an issue.

I recently had a case where in the middle of the divorce, my client's wife — who was to be sharing custody of the children — quit her job, left her children, and moved from Michigan to Oregon to be with an old high school flame she'd reconnected with on Facebook. Needless to say, she lost custody. If she had waited until the divorce was over, there could have been a very different result regarding the custody arrangement.

The examples are endless.

DOS & DON'TS

Do not post messages or photos on Facebook that can come back to haunt you. If you are still married, that would include posting photos of a boyfriend or girlfriend. The whole world can see them, especially if they are compromising photos or show a lack of discretion.

Think twice before participating in intimate photos or videos – anytime. You would be amazed at how many people allow compromising photos or videos to be taken while the marriage is good. Later these same photos or videos can end up online and wreak havoc. Revenge porn sites are designed specifically so such photos and videos can be posted. Making these images public is a way to inflict more emotional pain on a soon-to-be ex-spouse and can also create issues regarding custody.

Be careful what you say in emails and texts. They are fair game in a divorce. If you question the appropriateness of saying something in an email or text, don't. Almost daily, I deal with problem emails, text messages, and postings not only involving my clients and their spouses, but also their children. Emails and Facebook posts can be used against you, serving as evidence in a hearing or trial regarding custody, alimony, and division of property, where fault can influence the outcome.

Discretion is critical. Some attorneys tell their clients to close all Facebook and other social media accounts. It is often good advice, but most people in this age of social media will probably ignore it. Still, it's what I advise my clients. If you do post, be very careful about what you say.

Monitor your children. Kids' access to computers is often an issue in a divorce. For that reason, computers should be kept in a central area where adults can observe what's going on. Child predators are all over the Internet – and that can be a matter of life and death for your children. I've also had cases where children use obscene gestures online toward one parent with the knowledge and consent of the other parent. If one spouse is failing to monitor the children's activities on the Internet, or condoning bad behavior, it could become an issue in a custody dispute that has the other parent arguing lack of control or supervision.

Deleted doesn't mean gone. When you press the delete button on a text or email string, messages and images can still be retrieved. Companies that retrieve deleted items from computer hard drives are thriving. Subpoenas can be issued to search for deleted texts and depending on the length of time that has passed, and the technology, they can be retrievable. In several divorce cases I've handled, we were able to recover incriminating evidence even though it had been deleted.

In addition, emails can be a treasure trove of information in a divorce. I've seen emails that reveal an affair predating a divorce by months or years. Some, such as those about hiding assets or even plotting to leave a spouse, can be used as evidence in a divorce case.

WHAT'S LEGAL AND WHAT'S NOT?

There can be a tendency for a wronged spouse to feel that anything is fair game. That's not necessarily true.

Laws differ from state to state. In Michigan, for example, there is no requirement of physical separation during a divorce. Many other states require that spouses be separated before filing for divorce. Check with a local attorney for definitive advice.

By law, if you are snooping in your spouse's email account, and an email has been sent and opened, you're safe reading it. If the email is unopened, it is the same as opening a sealed letter. That's mail fraud, which can be a violation of criminal laws that apply to the Internet and email as well.

In one situation, a man was charged with hacking into a home computer during a divorce after forwarding emails his wife had sent to a prior husband regarding allegations of abuse concerning a child from her earlier marriage and the child he and his wife had together. Now, he had created the original email accounts for his wife and himself. The computer, a laptop and one of several in the home, was his. However, his wife lied and said that he did not use the computer in question. The first trial judge ruled that the emails were admissible in the divorce action and next, he was criminally charged with unauthorized use of the home computer. After a torturous battle of approximately one-and-a-half years, during which the prosecutor's office tried to force a plea deal, the client was ultimately exonerated with all criminal charges dropped before it went to trial. Sadly the fallout in that bitter divorce and custody battle continues.

Computer hacking, keystroking, and other spyware: against the law. I have had several cases where during a divorce, one spouse has activated devices that track keystrokes on a home computer. In some situations, that meant every email between myself and my client, the wife, was copied to her husband and his attorney. It's not only illegal, but also badly compromised attorney-client privilege and the relationship I had with my client. In these situations, the other side knew every step we planned to take before we even communicated with them. It was as if they already knew what our strategy was — and they did.

What do you do in a situation like this? You can contact the local police or prosecutor, though I have learned that they are reluctant to prosecute in these situations because resources are limited and crimes of violence, for example, come first.

Phone eavesdropping: it depends. Can you listen in on phone conversations? The laws differ from state to state. In some, phone tapping is totally illegal. In others, including Michigan, it can be legal if you are participating in the conversation even when the other spouse does not know that he or she is being recorded. I urge you to contact an attorney for more specific advice and information regarding the laws of your state should the issue arise in your divorce.

Tracking devices: generally illegal. Tracking devices on a car are illegal in many states. In some states, they are legal if they have been placed on the vehicle by a private investigator or a law enforcement officer. That is the law in Michigan. Prior to that change in the law, anyone could put a locator on a car.

However, smartphones can now be used as tracking devices. They are legal, though this is an area of the law that is constantly changing due to the radical changes in our highly technological world.

For example, I recently handled a case where a husband and wife shared a family plan for their iPhones. My client could view emails and also locate wherever his wife was through iCloud. Was it legal as a weapon in divorce proceedings? You must check with a local attorney because of the vast discrepancy in the laws in this arena.

Let's go back to Facebook. Recent studies show that it is now the "marriage killer," responsible for at least one out of every five divorces in the country.

The key is that Facebook entries, YouTube videos, email exchanges, tweets, texts, and pictures on social media that you may have considered private are discoverable and can be useful in a divorce or custody proceeding. They can be very important as evidence in custody disputes, as well as when fault comes into play over the division of assets or regarding alimony.

Facebook has privacy settings. Use them. You can defriend "frenemies" — those who may be monitoring your Facebook profile to give information to your estranged spouse.

Beware the video recording device. Some people use nanny cams and other video recording devices in their homes during a divorce. One client of mine was caught having sex with a boyfriend in the den of her home by her husband on video. It made the case difficult, to say the least.

The law holds that if a recording device is in a public place such as a living room or den, it can be legal. On the other hand, if it's in a bedroom or bathroom where you have a right to privacy, it is not.

Wrapping Up

The impact of social media, technology, and what you should and should not do in this age of cellphones and computers cannot be underestimated. Technology in this area is advancing much more rapidly than the law. Discuss these issues with your attorney as you proceed with your divorce.

Notes

Notes

_____

_____

_____

_____

_____

_____

_____

_____

_____

_____

_____

_____

_____

_____

_____

_____

_____

_____

_____

_____

_____

_____

_____

_____

_____

CHAPTER FIVE

Choosing an Attorney

If you are contemplating or going through a divorce, having the right attorney is critical. How do you select someone who is a good fit?

FAMILY LAW IS A SPECIALTY

In deciding whether to hire a particular lawyer, it is important to understand the role of the attorney in family law. It's a difficult specialty. In specializing in family law for 40 years, I have seen it grow from a marginal specialty to one where many of the finest attorneys gravitate. When I first started practicing, most attorneys did not specialize in any one area and dabbled in divorce. Their specialty was whatever their client happened to need. But over the years, family law has evolved significantly. It's become much more specialized and complicated for several reasons. A good family law attorney should be cognizant of the following key issues.

1. Whether dealing with divorce, child custody, or other aspects of family law, a family law attorney must know the laws in the state where he or she is practicing.

2. The attorney should also have at least a basic understanding of tax laws and related issues. This is especially critical when tax implications on property and alimony are factors. With thousands — even millions — of dollars at stake, the tax implications can be huge.

3. Knowing and understanding real estate is essential because many divorces involve residential, commercial, and vacation properties. In addition, following the recent recession, many homes were under water with negative equity. Decisions on whether it makes sense to keep or sell a home are common, and with drastically reduced values, it's not necessarily a simple decision. It's encouraging that as I write this book, real estate values are rising. I now have clients selling their homes in a matter of days at the listing price or higher.

4. Knowledge of basic business law, corporate issues, and how to handle a family-owned business can be critical. Fast food franchises and family-held businesses have been central to many divorces I've handled over the years.

5. An understanding of medical, dental, accounting, law, and other partnerships and professional practices is important. Different rules and strategies come into play with each.

6. A good divorce attorney will have strong knowledge of discovery, which is the means that attorneys use to make sure that you have a complete economic picture of your assets, liability, and income. It is impossible to achieve a good result without having a full and accurate assessment. Discovery is an area where many attorneys fall short, with sometimes grave consequences for clients. You need all of the pieces of the puzzle before you can achieve a good result.

7. Your attorney should be familiar with the judges, legal system, and key players in the jurisdiction where your divorce is going to take place. There is an old saying that a good attorney knows the law — and a great attorney knows your judge. Do not hesitate to ask how well your attorney knows the judges and other key players likely to be involved in your divorce.

8. When domestic violence is a factor, the attorney should be thoroughly familiar with the topic and aware of its nuances and repercussions. I recently took over a divorce where my client was told by her previous lawyer that psychological and emotional abuse did not count — only physical abuse mattered. That is clearly wrong; emotional and psychological abuse can be even more devastating than some forms of physical violence.

9. A good family law attorney is not a psychologist, but should have some understanding of psychology and human relationships. A tremendous psychological overlay permeates every aspect of a divorce and it can't be ignored. When clients come to a lawyer for help with a divorce, they are not happy — and that's only magnified by the end of the process. Think about it: You are a spouse who will end up with 50 percent or less of the marital assets, and often more debt, all while seeing your children a lot less than before. It is a very unhappy time.

   A good divorce attorney recognizes that sadness and devastation go hand in hand with most divorces. The lawyer also understands that there are no winners in a divorce. You want someone who is compassionate and understands that this is a difficult passage into a new phase of your life.

10. Having knowledge of child custody laws as well as the realities regarding custody and parenting time are critical. Your attorney should know that one size definitely does not fit all.

11. Not only should your lawyer be a good listener, empathy is important, too.

THE INITIAL CONSULTATION

How should you prepare for your first meeting with a prospective lawyer? Over the years, I've had clients walk in with many questions and a lot of information. More often, though, they arrive with no information and even less awareness of what they should be asking.

At the initial consultation, you and the attorney are both deciding if you would make a good fit to go forward — and if you are even ready to file for divorce. It's critical that you are comfortable with your lawyer, so don't hesitate to ask questions. Trust your gut reaction.

Some lawyers have an assistant meet with you on the first visit to take down the initial basic information. I prefer to do that myself. That way, I can get a feel for the case and the client as I begin establishing a relationship at the same time.

If you can, bring tax returns. Copies of investment, bank, and mortgage statements, along with a summary of credit card and other financial obligations, can be helpful. If you don't have this information, don't panic. It can be obtained as the case proceeds.

Be prepared to provide an attorney with a history of your marriage. I often ask a few basic questions: Why are you here? Is there any chance of saving your marriage?

I always suggest marriage counseling to see if there is any way to save the marriage before proceeding with divorce. Divorce should be the last resort — not the first.

Once I have the basics, I will ask about children and whether custody will be an issue. I will also discuss support and alimony issues.

Last but not least, we will review attorney fees. We'll get back to that later on in this chapter.

WHAT SHOULD YOU ASK?

The following questions are important when contemplating whether to hire an attorney.

1. *What percentage of your practice is devoted to family law?* You want a specialist to handle your divorce — not someone who dabbles in it. Too much is at stake.

2. *How long have you been practicing family law?* Experience is critical. It takes at least five years for an attorney to learn the basics of family law and the court system.

3. *Do you represent more men or women?* It is often better to have an

attorney who represents both men and women so that his or her practice is more balanced. Judges tend to respect someone who is not merely an advocate for one gender over the other. Where I practice, some firms use a strategy of marketing themselves as only representing men or women. In reality, their attorneys are no different than others in terms of specialization or expertise.

4. *How well do you know the judges?* You do not want your attorney walking into court without knowledge of the judge and key personnel in the courtroom.

5. *Is there any reason why you are not comfortable representing me?* You don't want your attorney to be biased or judgmental. Your case is the most important thing going on in your life and you want to make sure that there is a comfort level with your attorney and your situation, especially if it is unusual. A good lawyer won't make moral or value judgments, but still has to make the best of the facts in your case. Family law is very fact driven, meaning the details of your case will be very important.

6. *What is the attorney fee and retainer?* This is an important question. You deserve to get the answers up front.

7. *If I reconcile, or if part of the retainer is not used, will I receive a partial refund?* Many attorneys do not give refunds. Ask to see the written retainer agreement in advance. Some will keep the entire retainer even if you and your spouse reconcile early on. I do not agree with keeping any unused portion of the retainer under these circumstances.

8. *What if I change attorneys?* Can I receive the unused portion of my retainer back? In many cases, the first attorney and client are not a good fit psychologically. In that case, the unused portion of the retainer should be refunded if you change to a new attorney.

9. *How many divorces have you tried?* While the goal is to settle your divorce, it is important to know that your attorney can go to trial if necessary.

10. *What is your attitude regarding negotiations and mediation?* You want an attorney who solves problems and does not create them. Some are clueless about settling cases, leading to an unnecessary trial

and tremendous emotional and economic expense. You also want an attorney who will disagree with you when necessary. A good attorney will step back and look at the big picture.

11. *Will you provide me with copies of all papers, documents, and pleadings that you receive or file in my divorce?* You should know everything that is going on — not be kept in the dark. Your file should be a duplicate of your attorney's.

12. *When I call or send an email, how long should it take for a response? What is reasonable?* Surveys have shown that clients would like a response within two or three hours. That may not be possible if your attorney is out of town or in a trial. A good attorney should respond to all emails and phone calls by the end of the day if possible. If he or she is going to be unavailable longer than that, an assistant should follow up instead. You deserve to know what is going on in your case.

13. *How long should my divorce take from start to finish?* Laws and practices vary from state to state. Some divorces are complete in a couple of months if everyone agrees and there are no children. When there are multiple issues and children, the case can take as long as a year and sometimes longer, depending on the rules and regulations of the state and how busy the court docket is.

14. *Will there be assistants or others working on my case?* A good family law attorney often has a team working to assist you, with different people charging different rates. It is important to know who will be working with the lead attorney on your case. In the area of divorce, it is hard to check references for the attorney because of confidentiality issues. When I am asked for references, I ask select prior clients for permission to be contacted by prospective clients. This is highly unusual, though, since many of my new clients are referred from previous clients.

Trust your gut, talk to friends and relatives, and don't hesitate to check credentials. There are many rating services and also some organizations whose members are among the leading matrimonial lawyers in the United States. Examples include the American Academy of Matrimonial Lawyers and The International Academy of Matrimonial Lawyers. *AVVO.com, Martindale-Hubbell.com, Lawyers.com, Bestlawyersinamerica.com*, and *Superlawyers.com* are among rating services to consult.

Last but not least, I advise prospective clients to write down questions and make sure that everything on their agenda is covered. There is no such thing as a stupid question.

WHAT ABOUT ATTORNEY FEES?

Retainers: The most common arrangement is to pay your lawyer a retainer against an hourly rate. Retainers and hourly fees vary, based on the experience of the lawyer and where he or she practices. An attorney in New York will charge a lot more than another in a small rural community, for example. In many cases, the retainer will end up covering the entire divorce. It just depends on the complexity of the case and how much time is involved.

Some attorneys charge more for court appearances than office time. Most bill for phone calls and email correspondence. Find out how that works. For example, most attorneys will charge for driving time to and from court, or to and from meetings. Don't hesitate to ask your attorney how fees are calculated.

By the way, some attorneys will take a nonrefundable retainer of perhaps $20,000 or more that does not count against the hourly rate. I have had many people complain bitterly about this fee arrangement.

Flat Fees: Some lawyers charge a flat fee no matter how much time is involved. I don't like them unless the case is very simple. If it becomes complicated, the attorney is going to be reluctant to give you a lot of time once the flat fee is exhausted and you may find you aren't getting the attention your case deserves. That can lead to a disastrous result that you will have to live with for many years after the divorce is final.

Unit Billing: Here, the client is billed based on units of time. For example, the fee for a court appearance is set at one rate regardless of how long it takes. Ditto for drafting certain documents and other functions that relate to your case. Attorneys often will say that unit billing is better because a task that takes a new attorney several hours will take an experienced attorney perhaps a fraction of that time. These are issues that should be discussed and explained at the beginning of any case.

Value-Added: Some attorneys charge what's called a value-added amount for a good result or for the fact that he or she is an expert. Is that fair? Not only is it often unreasonable, but also some top attorneys will take advantage of clients with such value-added approaches. I have handled divorces where my fee in a very complex, sophisticated divorce was half what the other attorney charged. It is important that you get what you pay for. Don't use your children's college education funds to pay for a divorce.

Regardless of financial arrangements, it is critical to have a written agreement that spells out the scope of what the attorney is to do and what the charges will be. And don't be penny-wise and pound-foolish. I have met with clients who tried to cut corners by going to a less expensive attorney and then lived to regret it. Remember that you often get what you pay for. The decisions that you make in your divorce will affect the rest of your life.

REASONABLE EXPECTATIONS

Finally, you want to make sure that your attorney is working for you – and not the other way around. You don't want a lawyer who is going to create problems and turn a simple divorce into a monster. I have seen that on so many occasions.

You also don't want an attorney who says, "I will take care of you and you should not worry," or who makes promises or guarantees outcomes that set unrealistic expectations – and set you up for disappointment. You and your attorney should function as a team to achieve a result that makes sense for you as you go through this traumatic time in your life.

Having the right attorney is critical. If you find that your attorney is causing problems or not meeting your expectations, there is nothing wrong with talking to another professional and getting a second opinion.

Wrapping Up

Before you choose an attorney, arm yourself with knowledge about what to expect, what he or she should know, and what you should ask about during the initial consultation — including cost.

Notes

CHAPTER SIX

Before You File

Deciding whether to file for a divorce is very painful. I once had a psychologist tell me that you cannot just dip your toe in the water. Either you are in or you are not. Or think of a dog, like a poodle, with a cropped tail. The tail doesn't get clipped a little at a time, repeatedly, until the right size is reached. No, the cropping is done in one fell swoop. That is a divorce.

Over the years, clients have often asked, "What can I do to prepare?" Following are some steps for anyone contemplating a divorce to consider before taking the plunge into the turbulent waters of a divorce.

1. **Have you tried marriage counseling?**

   If not, you should. There are three good reasons to seek counseling with a good therapist. The first is to see if your marriage can be saved and enhanced. Second, it's critical to build a support system for yourself. The third is to make sure you know as much as possible about yourself; you do not want to keep making the same mistakes in relationships.

   During my career, I have represented two women who were both 36 years old when they came to me to file for their sixth divorce. One of the two then came back a few years later for a divorce from husband number seven. She had found another man. I knew her well enough by then to tell her not to rush and to get whatever was going on out of her system before filing for another divorce. She refused to listen to me. A year later, she called me to say I had been right and that she had made a mistake. She had gone back to husband number seven, with whom she had decided to live, but they weren't going to remarry.

   You need to learn from your past. Without help, you will likely marry the same type of person again and again. The physical package may be different, but the psychological package will be the same. You do not want to trade one abusive partner for another or an alcoholic for a new spouse with a similar or different addiction. These conclusions are based on many years of experience, along with many conversations about these issues over the years with fellow attorneys and psychologists who also see the same patterns.

2. **Find out as much as you can about your family finances.**

   Obtain copies of your tax returns. Copy investment and brokerage account statements as well as your bank statements. These should include both checking and savings accounts. Having a picture of your credit card history is critical as well, especially when so many families are deeply in debt. The more you know about all of your family finances, the better off you will be in the event of a divorce.

If there is a cash business, can you track the cash? I have had cases with restaurants where there were two sets of books. Is there a safe? If there is, photograph and document everything in the safe, including any cash, gold, or jewelry by way of examples. If you don't know a lot about your family finances, don't panic – the information will be discoverable during the divorce process with the assistance of your attorney.

3. **Prepare a budget.**

What are your family finances? What do you need on a monthly basis to make ends meet? Are you working? Are you looking for work? How up to date is your resume? Have a plan in mind if you have not been in the job market. Maybe you have been home for a number of years raising children. Do you have marketable skills? Or do you need to go back to school? These are issues you should be exploring with your attorney should you decide to proceed with a divorce. For assistance, see my budget planner in Appendix A at the back of this book.

4. **Do you want to keep or sell your home?**

This is important, especially with so many homes having little equity or being underwater because people have mortgaged their homes with first mortgages and home equity loans, and market values have been fluctuating greatly these past several years because of our turbulent economy. Should your spouse keep the house? If you have children, this can have an impact on housing as well. Deciding whether to keep or sell your home is not only an economic decision, but often, an emotional one as well.

5. **Talk to an attorney.**

Over the years, I have met with people who were contemplating a divorce, but were not ready. It is important to know as much as possible about your options even if you are not ready to file for divorce. Meeting with an attorney is also a good way to start the process of identifying someone who is not only knowledgeable and experienced, but also to whom you can relate and who makes you feel comfortable.

6. **If you have children, consider an arrangement that makes sense for custody.**

Are you and your spouse actively involved in the upbringing and raising of your children? Are both parents good with the children? Should you and your spouse have some form of joint or shared custody? Keep track of the activities and amount of time that you and your spouse each spend with your children. What are your respective roles as parents? In most states, child custody is based on what is in the best interests of your children. That can be difficult with all of the emotion involved in a divorce, but try to step back. Think about not what you want or what your spouse wants and instead evaluate what makes the most sense and what is in the best interests of your child or children. It is important that the result is one where your children feel safe and secure and are free to be loved by each parent even though the family relationship will be very different.

7. **Keep a diary.**

I believe in keeping a journal or diary for several reasons. First, it is a way to keep track of what is going on in your marriage. Second, it is important to document incidents as they occur.

When custody is an issue, keeping a journal is critical to show what is going on between you and your spouse and the children as well as to keep track of how much time each of you actually spend with your children – and how that time is spent.

Maintaining a journal is also helpful to your lawyer as you build a case, especially if there are hearings or trials months down the road. I don't know about you, but if you ask my wife, she would say that I don't remember what happened an hour ago, much less several weeks or months back.

Be sure to keep your diary in a safe, secure place so that you will have all of the information at your fingertips if you decide to proceed with the divorce. Since these are your intimate thoughts, you do not want to store it in a place where it can be found by your spouse. That would include the computer — especially if it is one that is easily accessible by other family members.

8. **As you prepare for a divorce, it is important to keep track of photos, emails, text messages, Facebook accounts, and other forms of electronic communication.**

You would be amazed at how much of a treasure trove the Internet and social media have become. I've had numerous cases where, via pictures, emails, or texts, one spouse has learned that the other has been cheating. Be careful what you do or say, especially if you are considering a divorce.

9. Come up with a plan for the future.

Where do you want to be in six months? A year? Five years? Ten? Do you want to work on your marriage? If you are close to becoming an empty nester, do you want to share your home, your bedroom – your life – with the man or woman you married and had children with? Do you have a foundation to build on? Have you reached a bump in the road that can be smoothed out? Is your marriage one of ships passing in the night? Are you intimate strangers? Do you hate your husband or wife? These are all questions to contemplate with care.

Remember that divorce is not necessarily the answer. And if you are having an affair, be careful. I have seen so many people leave one marriage for another, and then come back for another divorce. Do not trade one set of problems for another.

These are some of the most important decisions that you will be making in your life. Do not act impulsively and do not take them lightly.

A number of years ago, a woman came to me for divorce advice. She was 38 and her husband was having an affair. Ten years later, she came back and filed for divorce. This time she had a boyfriend and was ready to end her marriage. Try not to make a rash decision, but also don't procrastinate when you are in a terrible marriage.

10. Build a support system.

This is important. Who can you trust? Who among your family and friends can you confide in?

It is imperative to have a confidant to express your feelings and thoughts to – someone who can be your sounding board. Bear in mind that no one else can walk in your shoes or live your life for you. A lot of friends or relatives will provide well-meaning advice, but you are the one who has to live with the decision. Only you can make the final decision as to whether to end your marriage.

Also, be careful who you confide in. In several recent cases, my client's confidant was a double agent reporting back to the husband throughout the divorce. Make sure that you know who your friends really are.

11. Talk to your spouse.

Try to communicate. Saving your marriage should be your first option and filing for divorce your last. Is that a possibility?

You have to work on your problems. Having a therapist is critical because a trained third party who is not caught in the middle of your marital issues can help you sort things out and truly see if there is something to work on and save. I have so many people who come to me and say that they will not see a marriage counselor or believe that no third party can fix the problems. That is not good. If your marriage is in trouble, don't let pride stand in the way of seeking some objective help. I see so many marriages where one party refuses to see a therapist and have any outside intervention. That's often the last straw for the other spouse.

Some people try a separation. I believe trial separations rarely work and more often than not, ultimately lead to divorce.

Either way, it is important to weigh all options carefully.

12. Keep a file

Once you have decided to file for a divorce, it is important to set up and maintain a file of all of your notes and court documents. It should include anything that you receive from and send to your attorney so that as your case proceeds, you will have everything organized and at your fingertips. This will be helpful to you as well as to your attorney as issues arise. And being as organized as possible will help you focus on your divorce.

13. Finally, carefully evaluate your situation.

Are you sure that divorce is the only answer? Is the timing right? Think about all of the other issues I have raised in this chapter and make sure your decision is being made carefully and not as a knee-jerk reaction to a problem. If you are involved in or thinking about another relationship, be very careful. Forbidden fruit is wonderful, but that passion fizzles once your divorce has been finalized. Be careful what you wish for. Be true to yourself — and to your children.

Wrapping Up

Before you file for divorce, there's important work to be done. Marriage counseling, doing your homework, planning ahead, and carefully weighing all of your options are essential before you decide whether to divorce. Remember: Knowledge is power.

Notes

CHAPTER SEVEN

To File Or Not To File

1
2
3
4
5
6
7
8
9
10
11
12
13
14
15
16
17
18
19
20
21

In my many years of practice, a new client often wants to know: Does it matter who files first?

There is no easy answer.

Filing for divorce is merely the beginning of the legal process. Some attorneys specialize in marketing to a male clientele and others to women. In ads and commercials, they stress that it's important to be the one who files first. These are just gimmicks. I have called some of these law firms and was told that it is critical to file first for divorce to preserve your rights and gain the edge in divorce litigation. These firms often use fear tactics and high pressure to have you file for divorce first. Why? They want to be retained. They want your money!

Truth is, in most cases it does not matter who files first. Judges do not care. In fact, unless you are in court again and again with a very contentious, high-conflict divorce, the judges will not even know who you are.

I tell my clients that if they don't want a divorce, don't file. Many people come to me because their spouse is having an affair or wants out. I have found that often the spouse who is having an affair is not the one who files, instead pushing his or her spouse to file first. Then he or she can go to friends and relatives and say, "My wife has filed for divorce, look what she is doing! She is destroying our family!" It shifts the psychological burden of guilt from the wrongdoer, who becomes the object of sympathy. I have seen this happen time and again.

WHEN FILING FIRST MATTERS

Now, there are some cases where it is important to file first. Following are a few examples.

- A recent client and his wife were nationals from the United Kingdom. Their two children were born in the United States and held dual citizenship. The husband was here for his job and wanted to stay, while his wife wanted to take the children and return to Scotland. The marriage was clearly over.

  We filed first and obtained an order that the children could not be removed from the state where they were currently residing and could not go out of the country without a further order from the court. My client also took possession of the passports. With this immediate interim order setting custody and stating that the children could not leave the state, we took control of the case. The wife who very badly wanted to return to Scotland with the children was forced to negotiate because she could not leave with the children.

  In the end, we were able to achieve a quick resolution of custody and parenting time issues with the result that my client's wife was allowed to return to Scotland with the boys, while my client was able to have extended time with his children for many weeks at a time, both in the U.S. and Scotland. Based on this agreement, a court order was entered that protected everyone. This is a case where filing first put us in a position to negotiate a quick and fair result of all of the child-related issues in the divorce.

• It may be important to file first if your husband or wife is taking money out of savings or investment accounts or trying to hide assets. In this situation, you can petition the court to enter an order – typically called a mutual restraining order – simultaneous with the filing of the divorce complaint. Most judges will sign and enter an order that neither party can transfer or dispose of any assets while the divorce is pending or until further order of the court. This preserves the marital assets and starts the case with a level playing field.

• Another reason to file first is when domestic violence is an issue. It's important to have court protection for the abused spouse in place immediately. Courts will grant this type of protection. (Look for more on this topic in a later chapter.)

• It is critical to file first in situations where a spouse needs financial support and the other party has stopped paying the bills or bringing home a paycheck. By filing first, the person who needs the support can obtain an immediate "status quo" order to require the spouse who has stopped paying the bills or depositing a paycheck into a joint checking account to start paying the bills again and to maintain the terms that existed before the divorce was filed. This is often granted to make sure that one spouse is not trying to starve the other out by cutting off support. There can also be orders for child support – and in some situations, alimony – entered with the court at the beginning of a divorce under the appropriate circumstances.

• And then we have what I call the Stealth Divorce – divorces that are handled in complete secrecy and come as a total surprise. A prime example is the divorce between Katie Holmes and Tom Cruise. Holmes' father is a divorce attorney in Toledo, Ohio. She was clearly unhappy in her marriage. Cruise is one of the most powerful and successful actors in Hollywood. His home base and power center is in Los Angeles. He is also very active in Scientology, which is based in Los Angeles as well. Had the divorce been filed in California, Holmes would have had a distinct disadvantage.

With her father in control, Holmes set the stage. Every state has residency requirements before a divorce may be filed, and she and her daughter established residency in New York. She had security and a team of lawyers in New York City in place. While Cruise was on location shooting a movie out of the country, she filed for divorce. The attorneys obtained an order giving her interim custody of their daughter. Totally blindsided, Cruise then filed for divorce in California. To their credit and that of their attorneys, the entire case was settled in 11 days.

By filing first, Holmes and her father with their team of attorneys took control of the case in New York. By law, if there are two possible states where there can be jurisdiction to file for divorce, the first to file takes control and has go-ahead to proceed with the case. (This is an area where state laws can differ and local advice is critical.) Since Holmes filed first in New York, the case would continue there and the California case would be dismissed. There was a strong prenuptial agreement in place and more than enough money to go around. The key issue was the custody of their daughter. To their credit and that of their attorneys, they were able to stay out of the press and work out a private settlement with Holmes having primary custody in New York and Cruise having substantial time with their daughter as well. It turned out to be a win-win situation for everyone. This should be the goal in every divorce. I will reiterate throughout this book that your divorce is no one else's business!

EXPLORE ALL OPTIONS

Back to the question: To file first or not? In most cases, it doesn't matter. In some, it can be essential. Talk to your attorney and explore all options in advance. Pre-divorce planning can be critical to achieve the best possible result.

So the best answer is — it depends.

Wrapping Up

In most cases, it doesn't matter who files first in a divorce. Typically, the decision is based more on gaining a strategic or psychological edge than by a legal need to be the first to file.

Notes

CHAPTER EIGHT

Same-Sex Issues

Not long ago, I participated in a panel discussion on marriage and why so many fail. Other panel members included representatives from the Catholic Church, family therapists, and a rabbi.

At one point in the discussion, I raised the issue of same-sex marriages and why they should be legal everywhere. I stated that we are all different and the reason some of us are gay or lesbian is because of how our brains are wired. It's genetics — nothing more. My position was met with shock and strong disagreement from Catholic Church representatives and others with some strong religious beliefs.

Now, I have thought about this issue a lot. Who we are is due to genetics. We can be born with blue eyes or brown, fair skin or dark. There are endless genetic possibilities and combinations.

Whether we are gay, lesbian, or heterosexual is also a matter of genetics. It has been scientifically proven.

Sadly, even though the U.S. Constitution calls for separation of church and state, religion plays a very important role in our society. There are still many hot-button issues in which religion should be playing a secondary — not primary — role.

STRUGGLE FOR EQUALITY

Like in the 1960s when African-Americans and other members of our society fought for civil rights, there is now a struggle for equality on behalf of the gay and lesbian community.

As this book is being written, more than half of the states plus Washington, D.C., have made marriage equality the law. Those numbers are fluid, though, as many states with same-sex marriage bans face court challenges and appeals of previous decisions.

Still, many loving couples are being denied the right to marry; to have the legal benefits of spouses through inheritance and Social Security, medical, pension, and other benefits; and to legally adopt and share in the upbringing of their children. In states where same-sex marriages are legal, issues regarding property division, alimony, child custody, visitation, and child support are handled in the same fashion for all divorcing couples — heterosexual or not.

CIVIL ACTION

I have dealt with this issue in several cases over the years. In one case, two highly regarded therapists married in a commitment ceremony that had no legal standing. They shared their incomes and property and then the relationship went bad. In that situation, what could be done? They were not legally married and therefore could not file for a divorce.

The solution that I came up with was to file a civil lawsuit based on misrepresentations and financial mismanagement. There were no children, so it was all about money and real estate as well as issues over professional corporations and practices.

To say the least, it was a mess. There was a lot of anger and bitterness by my client and her partner just as there is in so many other divorces.

With skilled mediation, a settlement was finally reached, but it was much more difficult because it was not treated as a divorce and was not a family court case. A very positive factor was that the judge on our case understood the emotional dynamics and gave everyone a lot of latitude to mediate the case – to treat it more like a divorce than a fraud or undue influence case.

WHAT ABOUT KIDS?

When children are involved, there are other complications. In the majority of states that still ban same-sex marriages, one parent does not have any legal rights to a child who is legally adopted by or born to the other parent when the relationship goes sour. The laws are changing, and the trend is clearly toward the legalization of same-sex marriages.

However, there remain a lot of questions without good answers in states such as Michigan.

These include:
• The dissolution of a relationship that is not recognized.
• The handling of child-related issues.
• Social Security and pensions.
• Medical insurance.

BEING PROACTIVE

That's why creativity is critical. Same-sex couples should discuss what happens to children, property, support, and other income-related issues should the relationship end, and draw up formal agreements. I have drafted such documents over the years and can't emphasize their importance enough. Any experienced family law attorney can handle these agreements.

Other issues that need to be addressed include what happens to the validity of a marriage that is entered into in a state where they are legal when the same-sex couple moves to another state that still bans same-sex marriage?

What happens when a legal marriage is to be dissolved in a state that does not recognize them? Is there to be full faith and credit? Is the fact that the marriage is illegal in that state the overriding factor?

This is an area where change is long overdue. It's coming. More and more people favor same-sex marriage. The courts are coming around, even though many of our state governmental authorities haven't.

But think of it. If marriage for everyone would be legal throughout the United States from a civil perspective, then many of these problems would disappear.

Same-sex couples should be entitled to the same rights as anyone else. Or, as a well-known comedian recently said in explaining that he favors the legalization of same-sex marriage, they should have the same right to be as miserable as heterosexual couples.

Wrapping Up

When it comes to divorce, same-sex marriages are viewed the same as heterosexual marriages in states where same-sex marriage is legal. In those where it isn't, the picture is much murkier, with no provisions for issues like property division, alimony, or child custody, visitation, and support. State by state, the law is constantly changing. It should be in front of the United States Supreme Court in the near future.

My thanks to family law attorney Richard Roane for his comments and assistance with this chapter.

Notes

_____

_____

_____

_____

_____

_____

_____

_____

_____

_____

_____

_____

_____

_____

_____

_____

_____

_____

_____

_____

_____

_____

CHAPTER NINE

Cultural Issues

I practice family law in the Detroit metropolitan area, which has very diverse ethnic, religious, and racial demographics. As a family law practitioner, I believe it is necessary to address the wide variety of differences in the needs of a diverse religious, ethnic, and cultural population.

One of the judges where I practice is of Islamic faith. Early in her career, she dressed like any other judge. A couple of years ago, she started wearing a hijab, or head covering. She and I discussed it and she said her religion is important and that covering her head is a symbol of purity.

On any given day, there typically are many other members of the Islamic faith in her courtroom, as well as other litigants representing other religious, racial, and ethnic backgrounds going through divorce.

She told me that she gives people time and listens because how people express themselves varies among cultures. For example, a couple from Africa were very loud while speaking in court. By letting them proceed in that manner, she made it possible for them to communicate in a way that was normal to them, though perhaps foreign to us. She knows that listening and trying to account for cultural, religious, racial, and ethnic differences is very important in family law, and I agree.

CHANGING DEMOGRAPHICS

Twenty-five years ago, the majority of people I represented in divorce and other family law matters were born in America. Few cases involved people who had not lived in the United States for at least one or two generations. Times have changed significantly — and so has the cultural population of people experiencing divorce in most major U.S. metropolitan areas.

We are a cultural melting pot — a United Nations, really. Using metro Detroit as an example, we have one of the largest Arab populations outside of the Middle East. There are huge Hispanic and Chaldean communities, along with thousands of people who were born and raised in India and Pakistan, who may be Muslim or Hindu or Sikh — each sect with its own issues and attributes. Many come from Africa. The region has also become a major immigration point for thousands from the former Soviet Union and other parts of Eastern Europe.

And because Detroit is home to many large players in the auto and computer industries, it's common to see people from Japan, China, Korea, Thailand, and other parts of the Far East relocate here. That also tends to be true in most other large metropolitan areas or cities where technology is an important part of the economy.

Not surprisingly, then, I have represented people from many religious, ethnic, cultural, and racial backgrounds — some of them cultures in which, until recently, divorce was extremely rare.

In numerous cases, people come from societies where arranged marriages are common. Lifestyles and marital relationships that are accepted in other countries are often unsuccessful here, resulting in the dissolution of many arranged marriages.

For example, I have handled several cases with arranged marriages from India. If these couples were still in India, they probably would not be seeking a divorce. Here, with so many different lifestyles and attitudes, divorce becomes a more viable option. This happens more and more frequently.

CULTURAL BACKGROUND COUNTS

As an attorney, I know it is important to examine the differences and try to learn from them. When I first meet with a client, I make it a goal to not only gather the facts about the marriage and its problems, as well as the assets, liabilities, and issues, but also to familiarize myself with the client's ethnic and cultural background.

For example, how does the Muslim religion influence a divorce? How does the fact that women, in most Muslim countries, are treated differently from American women affect a divorce? How does the traditional attitude of the Muslim male come into play? All are relevant.

Muslim holidays are also critical to Islamic participants in a divorce. During these holidays, parenting time matters a great deal and needs to be respected and considered in the divorce judgment. This is also true of many Indians and various Hindu holidays.

Issues regarding immigration can frequently arise. Allegations of misrepresentation in which one party is said to have married the other party simply to obtain a green card are common. I have litigated numerous cases where green cards, student visas, and other immigration issues become entwined with the divorce. In these situations, it is important to bring in an attorney who specializes in immigration law. These are all delicate matters that call for sensitivity and attention.

IMPLICATIONS FOR CUSTODY

Custody issues can have unique considerations as well. If a parent disappears with a child to certain countries in the Middle East, for example, as well as to some other parts of the world that are not signatories to the Hague Convention regarding international child abduction, there is no reciprocity and it is impossible to have a child returned if the absent parent refuses.

Female roles in the Middle East and much of the Far East can differ greatly from those in the United States. In some cultures, women are still expected to remain in the home and defer to their husbands; they may not be active in the community or hold employment. I have also represented many clients where in-laws from a foreign country would move in and take over the child rearing or create constant conflict with a daughter- or son-in-law.

It is more and more common for people to marry into other faiths. If the marriage breaks down, the religious upbringing of the children can become a battleground.

I have had cases where one spouse has converted to the other's religion only to revert to his or her original faith once the marriage has disintegrated. These situations often turn ugly — and often, children become the victims caught in the middle.

I have had situations where a wife converted from Catholicism to Judaism and then back to Catholicism, leading to battles over holidays and parenting time. In some cases, parents are members of the same religion, but cannot agree on which church, synagogue, mosque, or temple that the children should attend. One time, a rabbi was called to testify as to which holidays were the most important for visitation/parenting time purposes.

In fact, I have been involved in many complicated and hard-fought custody battles, where both parents feel that they are capable of and entitled to joint legal and physical custody. To say the least, these situations can become complicated.

As an attorney, it is important to listen to my clients and try to understand their background and its implications. These extremely sensitive issues must be recognized and considered carefully when determining the best strategy for each client. Every case is unique and deserves a different approach. Extra attention on my part will result in a more satisfied client.

OTHER FACTORS

It is common for clients with successful businesses to deal in a lot of cash. Many foreign-born immigrants have become successful entrepreneurs in operations like liquor and party stores, small groceries, restaurants, and gas stations. This can make the discovery process to identify assets and debts extremely difficult. (For more on discovery, see Chapter Fifteen.)

Language can also be an obstacle. The American vernacular and connotations of American words are frequently confusing and frightening to people who have not been raised here. There is no assuming that our slang and idioms make sense to foreign-born clients. In depositions and courtrooms, interpreters can become critical when a client or witness speaks little or no English.

Wrapping Up

It is important for a client from a foreign country or distinct cultural background to make sure that his or her attorney is sensitive to the intricacies of a divorce that has cultural or ethnic considerations. We are all a product of our environment and our cultural and ethnic identities can mean a great deal to us. The exact same set of circumstances can be interpreted in a variety of ways, depending on the heritage and background of a client. An attorney must be not only knowledgeable, but also compassionate.

Satisfying the specific needs of our clients during the difficult time of a divorce not only makes one a better lawyer, but also a better, more empathetic human being. As the judge I mentioned at the beginning of this chapter so aptly stated, we can't ignore people's backgrounds. In family law, nothing is black and white.

We are all products of our environment.

Notes

CHAPTER TEN

The First Legal Steps

When you build a house, it all starts with the foundation.

In divorce, the foundation is the initial complaint or document putting your spouse on notice that you want a divorce.

In some states, the parties must reside separately and apart for a year before a divorce can be filed. In others, including Michigan, the husband and wife can not only live together throughout the divorce — and commonly do — but they also can be totally civil and even remain sexually intimate during the divorce process.

I have had many cases where throughout the divorce process, the relationship is off and on again and again while the couple attempts to decide whether to proceed with their divorce. This can be very confusing, especially to children.

It's best to check with an attorney where you live for the legal requirements and ramifications relating to this issue.

FILING THE COMPLAINT

In some states, the complaint will be a petition for the dissolution of a marriage: In the Matter of Jane Smith and John Smith, for example. In many other states, the laws require that there be a plaintiff, who is the person filing for divorce, and a defendant, or the person being sued for divorce.

The result is that the first pleading will be Jane Smith, Plaintiff vs. John Smith, Defendant. I prefer having it called in the matter of Jane and John Smith because it is less adversarial. Again, it depends on the laws and customs of your state.

The complaint should meet the legal requirements for a divorce in the state in which it is filed, but should not include a lot of information intended to inflame the divorce or embarrass the spouse. In most states, divorce filings are public and your personal lives should be kept out of court as much as possible.

The goal is to try to handle the process with dignity, demonstrating as much respect to your spouse as possible. In some situations, this proves impossible and then you have total warfare with no winners except the attorneys, who will be charging a lot more money.

With the complaint comes a document called a summons. This paper states that you have been served with a complaint or petition requesting a divorce and gives the respondent or defendant so many days — typically 21 — to respond. It is summoning you to take action or be in default. If you are the defendant, this is the time to immediately contact a family law attorney, if you haven't already, to find out what your legal rights are and what you should do next.

EX PARTE ORDERS

In many cases, some original orders go along with the initial complaint or petition. These are called *ex parte* orders, entered on behalf of the plaintiff. Based on the complaint that has been filed, it's a request in the divorce petition or complaint for a specific purpose, with immediate relief that can be granted without a hearing.

I typically use an asset injunction or restraining order. This is an order putting your spouse on notice that no money is to be removed from bank accounts, no assets are to be taken, and no insurance is to be changed. The reason for the restraining order or asset injunction, which is normally mutual, is to maintain a level playing field as the divorce proceeds and make sure that neither spouse is taking advantage of the other by removing or transferring funds or changing life or medical insurance beneficiaries.

I have had cases where one spouse or the other starts transferring or disposing of property. I have also seen a husband or wife start running up large credit card debts when he or she finds out that a divorce is being filed or about to happen.

In a recent case, one of the parties tried to prepay his daughter's four-year college education — $250,000 — and also tried to repay loans that he claimed were due to his father in the amount of $75,000. I have experienced situations where one spouse or the other would try to liquidate a retirement or money market account. Needless to say, the court stopped all of this.

The purpose of a restraining order is to stop these practices and make sure that property doesn't disappear. Such orders should be used in every divorce. That way, there is no question about maintaining the status quo regarding assets, debts, and insurance.

Last but not least, domestic violence is a factor in some divorces. In some states, there will be an order regarding the protection of the victim spouse — a personal restraining order, a personal protection order, or some similar type of legal device.

In some states, a separate legal action for a personal protection or similar order is required; in others, it can be part of the divorce. These are very important in cases where there has been a history of domestic violence or the threat of violence. These issues should be fully discussed with your attorney at the initial meeting.

INTERIM ORDERS

Other possible orders include those issued on an interim basis regarding child custody. I only use these in cases where one parent is threatening to remove the children from the home, state, or country. In cases where the children have already been taken, an interim order can be needed to require the immediate return of the children.

I generally recommend that both spouses continue the custodial arrangement they had prior to the initiation of divorce proceedings unless there is some type of serious problem. In Michigan, most courts will not issue an interim custody order if both spouses remain living together with the children.

Laws and rules regarding *ex parte*, interim orders are going to differ from state to state. To obtain an *ex parte* order, you must state in the divorce complaint or petition why it is imperative that an order be entered at once without a hearing and give examples.

In some cases, an interim order is put into place along with the original filing setting child support; a status quo regarding the payment of marital obligations such as the mortgage, utilities, and other expenses; or even the setting of alimony in some instances. These orders can differ from state to state — even county to county and attorney to attorney, depending upon the facts of your divorce and the traditions, laws, and rules where you live and file for divorce.

SERVING PAPERS

In many cases, divorce papers are delivered using a process server, a public official, or someone else who is legally able to serve the papers. My philosophy is to encourage the other party to accept the papers without the need for formal service.

Why? Because being served with divorce papers — especially at work or in a public place — can be embarrassing. Getting served at home, especially if children are there, can be humiliating — and upsetting to everyone.

To avoid this, I ask clients to talk to their spouses, explain that a divorce is being filed, and ask if they will accept the papers by mail delivery to the home. Normally a husband cannot serve his wife or vice versa. However, establishing an acceptance of service agreement in advance to sign for and acknowledge the papers eliminates the need for a process server.

I had a case where my client was having an affair. However, he had neglected to inform me of this salient fact. The wife was extremely angry, and her attorney wanted to have him caught in the act and served at a motel where he had been meeting with his girlfriend. This only adds fuel to the fire and is not a good way to start a divorce.

In other situations, I try to find out if another attorney has already been retained. With permission from my client and the knowledge of the other party, I will arrange for the other attorney to accept service on behalf of the other spouse.

That lowers the level of acrimony and embarrassment, the goal being to set a non-adversarial, cooperative tone from the outset. Divorces are painful enough without attorneys making it worse in the way that they handle the initial paperwork.

TROLLING

Where I practice, an issue known as "trolling" has reared its ugly head. In trolling, lawyers obtain a list of divorce filings from the courthouse where your divorce has been filed. They then send a letter informing your spouse that a divorce has been filed against him or her. The letter requests that your spouse contact the attorney for possible representation in the upcoming divorce action.

I find this tactic reprehensible for several reasons:

1. In some cases, papers may be filed, but service is being delayed for the following possible reasons: a special family event such as a birthday, wedding, or graduation; illness; or a long-planned vacation.

2. There could be minor children involved and the spouse who is filing may want to meet with the other spouse prior to service, to discuss ways of moving forward in an amicable fashion as well as how to tell the children.

3. Sometimes a spouse will file and then reconsider or suggest marriage counseling to his or her spouse. Then the other spouse gets the trolling letter in the mail and all bets are off. I have seen this happen several times.

4. When there is domestic violence, the filing and service must be very carefully handled. A trolling letter can have tragic consequences.

5. Finally, it makes attorneys look like bottom feeders. I have found that trolling letters are universally viewed with disgust by clients who receive them.

ANSWERING THE COMPLAINT

Once a spouse is served with papers, the next step is for the defendant spouse to file a response or answer. In some situations, there may be a counterclaim or cross complaint filed by the other spouse seeking a divorce as well. The strategies will differ depending upon your own situation, who your attorney is, and where you live.

While the original papers are the divorce's foundation, the final judgment or settlement agreement represents the rest of the house, so to speak. It should cover every relevant issue and provides the steps for you and your spouse to follow going forward.

Following is a checklist that I use in my practice. It's designed to help my clients set goals and know what may or may not be important in their divorce. Bear in mind that this is not necessarily inclusive and is meant only as a general guide; some of the points will not be relevant to every case and may not be applicable in some states. The goal is just to get you thinking about possible options as you move ahead with your divorce and the rest of your life:

1. Counseling to save your marriage or to help build a support system as you go through the divorce
2. Choosing an attorney
3. Filing for divorce
4. The initial papers, including *ex parte* or temporary orders
5. Child-related issues including custody and parenting time/visitation

6. Child support
7. Medical insurance and uninsured medical, dental, and other health-related expenses regarding your children.
8. Extracurricular activities for your children, including the associated costs
9. College and private or parochial school expenses and issues
10. Alimony/spousal support
11. Medical insurance going forward for a spouse, if possible, through COBRA, a federal law that permits a former spouse to be kept on medical insurance for a maximum of three years if the other spouse is employed by a company with a minimum of 20 or more employees
12. Discovery issues, or techniques for learning exactly what assets and liabilities are in your marital estate
13. Property, including real estate holdings, personal property, investments, professional practices, and degrees
14. Businesses of all sizes, ranging from small family businesses to larger corporate entities
15. Cars, boats, toys
16. Collectibles
17. Savings accounts, stocks, bonds, and other investments
18. Retirement accounts including 401(k)s, IRAs, pensions, and other vehicles for future retirement
19. Furniture and furnishings including antiques
20. Issues involving gifts and inheritances
21. Debts including mortgages, home equity loans, credit cards, debts to relatives, auto loans, or leases, just to provide several examples
22. Tax issues
23. Life insurance
24. Attorney and expert fees
25. Security for a divorce settlement

Every state has its own laws and quirks. That's why it is so important to talk to an attorney where you live. The information provided here is general and will vary depending on your locale, the laws of your state, and the practices of your courts.

Wrapping Up

The complaint, interim orders, serving papers, and answering the complaint lay the foundation for a divorce. Follow my checklist to help you set goals and think about the options as you move forward with your divorce — and life.

Notes

CHAPTER ELEVEN

Alimony, aka Spousal Support

Many clients over the years have asked me if they are entitled to alimony as part of a divorce settlement. An equal number have stated unequivocally that they will never pay a dime of alimony to a soon-to-be former spouse.

Where I practice law, alimony is now called spousal support because it is intended as support for either spouse — husband or wife — as part of a divorce settlement or judgment.

Twenty years ago, it was rare for a wife to pay alimony to her husband. Today with many women working in high-paying fields and many husbands staying at home with the children, it's not uncommon for a husband to receive alimony from his wife.

I have represented some women doctors who were very upset when they learned that they would be paying alimony to their soon-to-be former husband. Recently, I mediated a case in which the wife's earnings were significantly higher than those of her husband, who had some psychological problems and was earning very little income.

However, he had a very large collection of memorabilia valued at around $200,000, including a mold of the Heisman Trophy. After negotiations back and forth, I suggested that he keep the entire collection in return for his wife having no obligation to pay alimony. Everyone accepted this proposal and the case settled.

In many divorces, alimony doesn't apply. There are plenty of others, however, in which alimony is going to be an obligation for many years.

CIRCUMSTANCES MATTER

In determining whether there will be alimony, attorneys and judges look at many factors.

Let's say you and your spouse have been married for just a few years. In that situation, the possibility of alimony is slim. In most short-term marriages, there is going to be little or no alimony unless there are unusual circumstances. One example where alimony might apply in a three- or four-year marriage could be when one spouse is still in school and needs alimony to help complete the course of study.

At the other end of the spectrum is the long-term marriage in which the wife has been home raising children and not worked in many years. In this situation, an order for some type of alimony is likely. The longer the marriage and the higher the income level, the stronger the likelihood that there will be alimony.

FOLLOWING ARE SOME FACTORS WORTH THINKING ABOUT.

1. **The length of your marriage.** The longer you are married, the more likely there will be alimony.

2. **Earning capability.** If you have been out of the job market for many years, that is going to be an important factor regarding alimony. If you are in a field where you need retraining or where your skills are obsolete, alimony is more likely.

3. **The source and amount of property awarded to you and your spouse.** If you and your husband or wife have a fairly equal division of property and there is not a lot of value on either side, then this will not be a factor in determining alimony. On the other hand, if one spouse receives a substantial settlement, this may be in return for no alimony.

   I have had many cases where one spouse receives a greater portion of the marital estate in return for little or no alimony. I have also had cases where my client, the husband, and I figured out approximately how much the alimony might be and instead, he agreed to pay his wife more money up front. I had one client pay his wife $2 million with the understanding that he would not be providing alimony.

   The thinking here is that a bird in hand is clearly worth more than two in the bush, especially when the future can be so uncertain. That's especially true in recent years, when the economy crashed and many highly paid executives and professionals lost their jobs. The economy has rebounded, but we have learned there is no guarantee in the job market. It used to be that someone would work for a major corporation until retirement. That is no longer the reality; change is the norm.

   Another situation might be where one spouse has a substantial inheritance; that could be an argument against alimony.

4. **Your age and that of your spouse.** The older you are, the more likely it is for some form of alimony. Someone in his or her 50s or 60s is going to have a much stronger case for alimony than people in their 30s or even 40s.

5. **Ability to pay alimony.** What is your income? What is your spouse's income? This is the next factor that should be looked at. Even in a long-term marriage, if the money isn't available, there will probably be little or no alimony.

6. **Current circumstances.** Are you or your spouse unemployed? Is someone about to finish his or her education? Are there still children growing up in the home? These are considerations as well.

7. **Assess your needs and those of your spouse.** Keeping a budget and trying to figure out what you will need to live on is important in trying to determine whether there will be some form of alimony.

8. **Health is an important factor.** Even in a short-term marriage, one of the parties suffering from severe health problems is clearly a factor. I have seen young clients who would normally not qualify for alimony become eligible

because of crippling injuries or a serious illness that makes it impossible to work. If it is a lifetime illness that is going to worsen over the years, even in a short-term marriage, long-term or even lifetime alimony may be critical.

I recently settled a divorce where my client had a stroke while in her 30s and could no longer work. Even though she was on disability, alimony was necessary. The husband fought this hard, but ultimately we settled with her receiving alimony until her death, remarriage, or some further order of the court. Her tragic health situation was a major issue, requiring alimony without any time limits.

9. **What is your prior standard of living?** If you have lived an affluent lifestyle for a number of years, that can be a factor for alimony. This does not mean that you will be able to live as well as before, unless there is an endless amount of money. Even sports figures and stars of stage or screen have to cut back when they are going through a divorce.

10. **Past conduct.** In some states, fault or your past relations and conduct can be a factor in the determination of alimony. If you have been spending a lot of money on a "friend" during the marriage, if there is a history of domestic violence, or if there are issues involving alcohol or drug abuse, for example, the courts can look at these as part of the equation in deciding whether there is going to be alimony as well as the amount and duration.

I happen to like alimony as a tool in divorce. First, alimony is taxable income to the spouse who is receiving it and tax deductible to the person paying it. If you are in a fairly high income tax bracket and your soon-to-be former husband or wife is in a much lower tax bracket, you can pay spousal support to your spouse with the government footing part of the bill.

Let me give you an example. Let's say that you are earning $100,000 per year. Let us also say that your spouse's annual income is $25,000. Every dollar that you spend in alimony is going to cost you 70 cents if you are in the 30 percent tax bracket. If your spouse is in a 20 percent tax bracket, it becomes a win-win situation for both of you, since she pays 20 cents in taxes on every dollar you pay. A good attorney will look at the tax aspects of alimony and try to structure a settlement that makes sense for everyone.

To meet IRS requirements and be tax-deductible, alimony must have at least one contingency as grounds for ending it. A very typical divorce judgment will state that alimony is payable for a number of years, but will end upon the death or remarriage of the spouse who is receiving it. There can be other situations where the alimony will only end upon the death of the spouse who is receiving it — not upon remarriage.

In some cases, alimony ceases upon the death of the person paying it as well. In that situation, life insurance or some type of security typically covers the loss of alimony for the recipient in the event of the untimely death of a former spouse.

The death-only clause is more common when alimony is being used as part of a buyout for the other spouse's interest in a business or professional practice, for example. Having it end upon remarriage would be unfair in that situation.

Another issue that I often face is where alimony is going to run until your soon-to-be former spouse's death, remarriage, or the further order of the court. Known as lifetime alimony, it's not very common. When it does happen, it is in a long-term marriage, where one spouse has always been the primary breadwinner and the other can never be competitive in the job market – usually a marriage of 30 or more years with a couple in their late 50s. What usually happens is that when the person paying the alimony retires, that can be a basis for lowering or eliminating the alimony, especially when Social Security or pensions come into play as a replacement for the alimony. In that way, lifetime alimony is not usually for life.

Another issue is the impact of retirement upon long-term alimony. I have had several cases where retirement either modified or terminated the alimony obligation. This should be planned for in your divorce negotiations and settlement agreement.

As you can see, alimony depends upon the circumstances of each case. It is not one size fits all and can be very useful in trying to structure a settlement that makes sense, taking into account the many factors that I have listed earlier in this chapter.

It is so important to have a good attorney to assist you with alimony issues because they can be very complex and it is important that they are properly handled so that both you and your spouse are fully protected.

NO SINGLE FORMULA

A final observation I have shared with many of my fellow attorneys and my clients is that alimony is highly subjective.

I have been in seminars where judges attending were surveyed as to how they handle alimony in several situations. The results have been astounding. Some judges recommend little or no alimony and others would grant fairly significant sums over a long period of years.

I also believe that women judges can be harder on the issue of alimony than their male counterparts. Some of the women judges where I practice agree that women should be treated equally and disagree with the paternalistic attitude pervasive in our family courts in the past. This is because they are working and often raising a family, have made it, and feel that other women should be able to work and make it as well. This view is shared by many attorneys I know who also specialize in family law.

Finally, it's important to keep an open mind about alimony because often, it can be a very helpful tool. Try not to think of it as paying for a dead horse, or a vacation long after you have returned. Instead, look at it as just another bill to pay, or a "cost of doing business" and moving on with your life.

Wrapping Up

It's important to know the factors that attorneys and judges look at regarding alimony and understand what constitutes reasonable expectations. Alimony can affect you and your soon-to-be former spouse's lives for many years after the divorce.

Notes

_____

_____

_____

_____

_____

_____

_____

_____

_____

_____

_____

_____

_____

_____

_____

_____

_____

_____

_____

_____

_____

_____

_____

CHAPTER TWELVE

Child Support

1
2
3
4
5
6
7
8
9
10
11
12
13
14
15
16
17
18
19
20
21

Financial support to help house, clothe, feed, and fund other expenses relating to raising children is mandated in every state. It is based on a computer-generated formula that differs slightly from state to state, and several factors are taken into account.

The formula includes both parents' income from all sources including wages, money that is income but goes into your IRA or 401(k) investment income, income from disability insurance, unemployment compensation, and Social Security.

The formula will look at the income from each parent as well as the number of children and the number of overnights that the children spend with each parent. Child support is not doubled for each of your children, but is generally based on a type of sliding scale formula. The child support formulas also include medical insurance and uninsured medical expenses for your children.

These formulas are easily accessible online in every state. You can obtain this information yourself or through a local attorney.

The easiest cases for determining the amount and setting child support are where both parents earn a paycheck from a company where all of their income is reported. The most difficult would be when one parent is self-employed or works in a business where a lot of the income is not being reported. These are the cases that give attorneys and the courts nightmares.

In some circumstances, a lifestyle analysis is employed to determine child support. Here, having a knowledgeable attorney can be critical. I have seen cases where a $300,000 house was purchased in cash, but the tax returns only showed an annual income of $50,000. Often, accountants are brought in when the income stream is hidden and complicated.

Payment of child support is normally done through the court system, typically through state-ordered funds or the arm of the court that deals with divorce involving minor children.

Once child support is determined, it is normally reviewed every three years. At any time, either party can request a modification based on changes in circumstances that can include the loss of a job, a reduction in earnings, or a tremendous increase in income.

FACTORS IN SUPPORT

The more overnights each parent has, the less child support that is going to be paid. To some extent, there is a balancing act between income and overnights.

If each parent has a comparable amount of income and share custody equally, there will be little or no child support. This is based on the rationale that each parent is supporting the children when they are with that parent.

On the other hand, if the parent who does not have a lot of overnights with the children has a much greater income than the parent who has the children most of the time, child support will be much greater.

When my client is the father and the major wage earner, who also wants as many overnights as possible with the children, I suggest this tradeoff: In exchange for more time with the children, he is willing to forego a substantial reduction in child support so that the economics, at least to some degree, can be kept out of the equation. Every situation is different, but I believe, as parents, you should avoid using child support as an economic weapon in your divorce. Sadly, I have seen and been involved in many cases where people are fighting about the number of overnights and seeking more time solely because it means paying less child support. The reality is that it is costly to raise a child and unless you are in a very high-income situation, the expenses are much greater than the amount of child support paid.

Over the years, some clients have asked me if they can require their soon-to-be ex-spouse to document where the money for child support is going. The answer is no. In the first place, it is impossible to determine where all of the money for support is going and in the second place, no court will allow such micromanagement.

Think of what child support is intended to cover: food, clothing, a portion of the mortgage payment or rent, part of the utilities, part of the costs of a car along with gas, maintenance, and insurance, as well as entertainment and all of the endless incidentals that go hand in hand with raising kids.

Too many people will not let go and move on, and child support can become a prime example of that. Do not try to micromanage your former spouse to try to determine where your child support is going. It will do you no good.

The tragedy of most divorces is that when there is a split, too often there is not enough money to go around. But as I often remind my clients, support is for your children. Before you become entrenched in a battle over support, remember that you want your child or children to be supported. Your children are caught in the middle of your divorce to begin with — you do not want them to go without the basic necessities.

In most states, child support usually ends when the kids reach the age of majority, 18, or finish high school, whichever is later. It is important to talk to your attorney or check the laws in your state for more specific information.

BEYOND SUPPORT

After the necessities, there are other expenses associated with raising children that will need to be addressed. When you are contemplating or going through a divorce, it is important to sit down with your spouse and discuss how these items will be handled going forward. If not, be sure to raise them with your attorney so that they will part of the negotiations and ultimate settlement. In some states, courts will not order payment for extracurricular activities; in others, they may.

In many of my cases, we may negotiate a separate paragraph to address sharing of costs for extracurricular activities over and above child support. These can include expenses for pursuits like dance, music lessons, and sports. Some activities are inexpensive, but when you get into situations such as hockey, dance, or figure skating, the costs can become tremendous. Boy Scouts, Girl Scouts, religious classes, and ceremonies can be counted in those extracurricular expenses. The list can be endless and these are just a few of the many possibilities.

Other child-related expenses that should be discussed include school if there is parochial or private schooling involved. Summer camps are often discussed and can be included as part of an overall financial settlement.

Day care is another component. These are normally addressed as part of the child support formula. In Michigan, for example, day care can be included – but only until a child reaches the age of 12. At that point, it is presumed that there is no longer a need for day care.

As for college expenses, they can be part of the divorce settlement in some states and can even be ordered by the trial judge. In Michigan, they cannot be ordered by the court.

I have negotiated many cases over the years where there is an agreement reached for either a sharing of college-related expenses or for one parent to pay part or all of the college costs. As long as they are part of the final negotiated settlement and divorce decree, they are full enforceable by the court and typically consist of tuition, room, board, and books.

In one Michigan case, college expenses were covered, but the college was not spelled out. That turned out to be a huge mistake on the part of the husband, who had agreed to pay them. The child was accepted at Harvard University and the father had to pay the tab. To avoid this type of problem, I usually include language that the costs of a college education shall be limited to the price of a four-year public in-state institution unless the parties agree otherwise. It should be noted, too, that few students finish a college degree in four years anymore.

Child support encompasses many issues and I urge you, as I do my clients, to step back and try to put your children's needs ahead of any anger or problems that you have with your spouse. You want to do what is best for your family – and that means not fighting over every dime of child support.

Wrapping Up

A variety of factors come into play to determine the rate of child support. Additional costs such as extracurricular activities and school expenses should also be considered.

Notes

CHAPTER THIRTEEN

Keeping A Journal

I have long advocated that my clients keep a journal or diary as they go through a divorce.

Why?

First, it is a way to keep track of events or incidents as you go through the painful divorce process. Rather than have clients call or email me every day, which can run up costs, I encourage them to write things down so we can discuss them at one time, or when there is a hearing or other event that is about to occur in the divorce. Also, as we prepare for a hearing, trial, or even mediation, I will have a record of all significant incidents or events. This way, things are fresh and can be easily put together at the appropriate time as we develop and prepare the case.

As you go through your divorce, there will often be incidents involving your children or spouse that are significant. For example if there is an argument, or a problem with one of your children, write down what happened, when, who was involved, and other specific details. This can be very important as you prepare for future court dates or other events. Some examples will include words you had with your spouse, confrontations regarding the children, threats over the phone, failing to keep an appointment, or anything out of the ordinary.

Keeping a journal can also be therapeutic. It is a way to get issues off your chest. And you can review the details later and see them in the cold light of another day.

It is also important in a custody case to keep track of the time you spend with your children and note what you are doing with them on a regular basis.

A journal is also the most accurate way to track events. If your divorce lasts for six months to a year or more, then your journal or diary will give you details of events that happened months ago and could be very important as part of the ultimate strategy and preparation for your divorce.

Of equal importance if you keep a divorce journal is making sure that it is in a safe place that cannot be accessed by your spouse, your spouse's allies, or attorney. The computer may be convenient, but it may be the worst place from a security or safety standpoint – especially if it is a family computer with access to everyone in the house.

I tell my clients to keep their journals in a safe place – not in your home and not in your car.

Several years ago, I handled a divorce where my client's husband had kept a journal of all of his affairs. This included his ratings of their sexual performance as well as of his wife's. My client, the wife, obtained a copy of this journal and it helped us a lot in obtaining a favorable resolution to the divorce case.

Be careful what you say or write, be careful where you say it, and make sure that whatever you have in a journal is kept in a very safe place and is shared with your attorney.

Wrapping Up

Keeping a journal helps you keep track of details and provides a record of events as you go through a divorce. The key is being brief: Stick to the who, what, where, and when. This creates an important building block for you and your attorney as you prepare your case and get ready for settlement and/or trial.

Notes

Notes

_____

_____

_____

_____

_____

_____

_____

_____

_____

_____

_____

_____

_____

_____

_____

_____

_____

_____

_____

_____

_____

_____

_____

_____

CHAPTER FOURTEEN

The Children

Children are the biggest losers in divorce. There are often no easy answers for them. They are innocent victims.

I have witnessed countless divorces involving children and have spoken to many therapists about this issue.

Even in the most horrible of marriages, children want their parents to stay together. This is their norm. They love and want to be with both parents. No matter how young or old your children are, they will be affected in some way. Even adult children experience the emotional fallout when their parents decide to divorce.

PARENTING TIME

If this book were being written 20 years ago, we would be dealing with a much more old-fashioned, traditional type of child custody. In many states, there was a "tender years" presumption in which the mother was favored for custody, especially with young children. Dad would typically see the children on alternate weekends and perhaps one evening a week for dinner. There would be a sharing of major holidays such as Thanksgiving, Christmas Eve, Christmas Day, Easter, Memorial Day, the Fourth of July, and Labor Day, alternated in some fashion on a yearly basis.

Mom would have the children on Mother's Day, Dad on Father's Day, with a sharing of or alternating the children's birthdays. Summer would be divided into blocks of time, with each parent having the right to a couple weeks' vacation. School breaks would be shared in some fashion as well.

It is a very different world today. In most states, the laws look at the children's best interests. Not only do fathers get custody often, but also some type of joint or shared custodial arrangement is common. Both parents usually work. The sharing of child rearing in more and more intact homes leads to a continued sharing at the time of a divorce.

In many of my cases, parents share time with the children on an almost equal basis. A typical schedule is called a 2-2-5; here, each parent will have two overnights every week and then the weekends alternate. For example, Mom will have every Monday and Tuesday overnight, Dad will have Wednesday and Thursday overnight, and the children will alternate weekends consisting of Friday, Saturday, and Sunday with each parent. The five in this equation refers to the fact that the children never go more than five overnights without seeing the other parent.

Other arrangements might call for one week on and one week off. In this scenario, the parent who doesn't have the children for the week might get them for a Wednesday overnight.

Many cases call for some type of shared custody, but not necessarily 50-

50. Maybe one parent has more time during the school year and the other more during the summer. Or Dad has alternate weekends from Friday until Monday and one overnight every week; that leaves Mom with nine overnights out of 14 and Dad with five.

Creativity is important, and the possibilities are endless. The main thing is to keep in mind what is best for the children – not the parents.

JOINT LEGAL CUSTODY

Your marriage may be ending, but you are still going to be parents together – for the rest of your lives. Many parents have joint legal custody, which includes sharing decision-making regarding your children going forward. The idea is that each parent fully participates, consistent with the best interests of the children.

That means you and your former spouse shall communicate – preferably by picking up the phone. If that does not work, communicate by email or text in an effort to amicably reach decisions that are in the best interests of your children.

In many of my high-conflict divorces, we actually spell out the times and means by which each parent will communicate with the children when they are with the other parent. This can be by Skype or phone, using computer programs such as Our Family Wizard, and by texting.

Each parent shall have the authority to make routine day-to-day decisions concerning the welfare of the child or children while in their care. These are normally spelled out in the final divorce judgment.

In addition, these are key points that are agreed upon:

1. Each parent shall exert reasonable effort to maintain free access and unhampered contact between the child and the other parent, including allowing telephone contact with the other party at least once a day during parenting time.

2. Neither parent shall do or say anything in the presence of the child or children, nor allow others to do so, that portrays the other party in a negative or false light, or that will tend to discredit or damage the love that exists between the child and other parent.

3. Consider the welfare and act for the ultimate good of the child or children at all times.

4. Never attempt to alienate a child from the other parent. Each spouse should acknowledge a duty to act so as to foster, encourage, and support a strong, loving relationship between the child and both parents.

5. Properly notify the other parent in the event of the illness of, or injury to, a child.

6. If either parent has knowledge of any circumstances seriously affecting

the health or welfare of the child, promptly notify the other parent.

7. Each parent shall also keep the other fully informed as to a child's medical status and educational progress, and each parent shall have full access to all school, medical, psychological, religious, and other pertinent records.

8. Each parent shall have the right and obligation to request and receive reports from third persons concerning the health, education, and welfare of the child, including school report cards.

9. Each parent shall cooperate and provide the other parent with copies of a child's report cards and sports activities schedule.

10. Each parent shall keep the other fully informed regarding any involvement of the child with proceedings of any court.

11. As parents, you shall each use your best efforts to work together to ensure consistency and agreement of matters affecting the upbringing of the child and to work together to promote the child's best interests.

12. Support each other in the enforcement of reasonable rules and expectations for the child.

13. Keep each other informed of the whereabouts of your child or children when they are within each parent's custody and control, including providing telephone numbers, full travel schedules, itineraries, and places of lodging.

14. Each parent shall notify the other parent of any travel plans involving the child as soon as he/she becomes aware of them.

15. Neither parent shall schedule activities for the child that interfere with the other parent's parenting time, except that each of you recognize and accept the fact that your child's sports and extracurricular activities may conflict with your parenting time.

16. Work together to reasonably share responsibility for the continued participation in sports and extracurricular activities.

17. Cooperate with respect to children so as to maximize and advance their health, emotional and physical well-being, and to give and afford the affection of both parents and a sense of security.

18. Neither parent will directly or indirectly influence the child so as to prejudice him or her against the other parent.

The preceding statements are typical of language that I include in my divorce judgments when minor children are involved, and they are words all parents should try to live by.

Over many years of handling divorce and custody cases, I have seen every one of these broken. I have dealt with cases where one parent will do everything possible to poison the relationship between the children and the other parent. I have seen examples of violence toward children, and countless cases of deliberate parental alienation by one parent toward the other. I have seen children who refused to see or talk to a parent because of multiple subtle (and not so subtle) attempts at alienation by the other parent — situations that are far too prevalent.

All I can say again and again is that while you are trying to hurt your soon-to-be former spouse in this way, you are really hurting your children and damaging them to the extent that they cannot form healthy relationships as they become adults. I am in a case now where there are false accusations by my client's former wife against his current wife. I have had cases where parents will do anything they can to hurt the other parent. The result is that they only cause problems — and often, permanent damage — to their children. In one situation, after years of parental alienation, a child killed himself when he turned 18.

Words, actions, gestures, and things said or not said can be horribly damaging to your children.

PHYSICAL CUSTODY

As I mentioned earlier, almost every state has some form of best interests of the child statute. I would like to share with you the Michigan Child Custody Act, which considers the best interests of the children in deciding custody and is similar to the laws in most states. It spells out the factors that courts must look at in deciding where children will live once the divorce is final.

1. The love, affection, and other emotional ties existing between the parties involved and the child.
2. The capacity and disposition of the parties involved to give the child love, affection, and guidance and continue the educating and raising of the child in the same religion or creed, if any.
3. The capacity and disposition of the parties involved to provide the child with food, clothing, medical care, or other remedial care recognized and permitted under the laws of the state in place of medical care, and other material needs.
4. The length of time the child has lived in a stable, satisfactory environment, and the desirability of maintaining continuity.
5. The permanence, as a family unit, of the existing or proposed custodial home or homes.
6. The moral fitness of the parties involved.
7. The mental and physical health of the parties involved.
8. The home, school, and community record of the child.
9. The reasonable preference of the child, if the court deems the child to be of sufficient age to express preference.

10. The willingness and ability of each of the parents to facilitate and encourage close and continuing parent-child relationships between the child and the other parent.
11. Domestic violence, regardless of whether the violence was directed against or witnessed by the child.
12. Any other factor considered by the court to be relevant to the particular child custody dispute.

In preparing a custody case for trial or settlement, these are the key factors that I build on with my clients.

In most divorces, the best approach is to sit down and try to work out a reasonable custodial and parenting time arrangement — one that makes sense for you and your children. This should take into account work schedules, traditions, and routines.

A question that I am often asked is at what age can a child decide where he or she wants to live? I tell my clients that the older the child, the more input he or she will have. There is no magic age. In some states, it may be 12 or 13.

While judges will listen, the ultimate decision is the court's when parents can't agree. I have had more than one judge tell me that no 14- or 15-year-old is going to tell them how to run their courtroom; if the parents can't work out a custodial arrangement that makes sense, the judge will make the determination for them.

And teenagers are like the 1,000-pound gorilla. Where they sit, they stay. I also have found over the years that when you are dealing with teens, it is often reverse custody: You take them; no, you take them. They are difficult and going through many physical and emotional changes. Pile a divorce on top of that and all hell can break loose.

Besides, older children want to spend most of their time with friends and school and extracurricular activities and less and less with either parent.

There is an old saying: Little children, little problems and big children, big problems. It is so true!

One caution: Children of all ages can be very manipulative, even when a marriage is intact. When Mom says no, the children will go to Dad — and vice versa. When you are divorced or going through a divorce and trying to curry favor with your children, know that they will play each of you against the other constantly. The less that you are able to communicate, the more that you are going to be played and manipulated by your children.

Wrapping Up

Parenting time, legal custody, and physical custody are top among the key issues that must be resolved when parents divorce. How to structure custody, communicate effectively, and make decisions regarding your children under such trying circumstances takes planning, thought, and willingness to negotiate, keeping in mind what is best for the children.

Notes

CHAPTER FIFTEEN

The Art Of Discovery

Discovery is the way to take stock of what you and your spouse have in your marital estate as well as identifying other issues involving your children.

Before a divorce settlement can be reached, it's imperative that everyone know what assets and liabilities there are to be divided. Think of a deck of cards. A full deck has 52 cards in it. In a perfect world, when you and your spouse are dividing property, you should each receive half, or 26 cards. What if your spouse is hiding some of the marital estate and there are only 50 cards? In that scenario, you would receive half of 50, or 25 cards, and your spouse would receive 27 cards – more than half.

In some cases, if a spouse is more devious and an attorney fails to do proper discovery, there may only be 46 cards. Then, you would only receive 23 cards and your spouse 29, which is an even greater disparity. This is why honesty and full disclosure through discovery is so critical.

I recently became involved in a case where a spouse failed to disclose his 401(k). He cashed it in during the divorce and no one knew about it. Now I am reopening the divorce because of this possible fraud. The 401(k) was more than $150,000, which is significant. His actions have deprived his spouse of at least $75,000. That's why being thorough during the divorce is critical.

AFFIDAVITS

When the marital estate is simple, perhaps consisting of a home, some savings, and retirement accounts such as 401(k)s or IRAs, along with some credit card debts, and a couple of cars, discovery can be simple. If the couple trust each other and are getting along, each spouse completes an affidavit listing all assets and liabilities under oath. This is protection in the event of an error or omission and serves as a basis to divide the marital estate without need for more formal discovery.

INTERROGATORIES

In the vast majority of divorces, the circumstances are more complicated and most attorneys will file interrogatories. These are requests for information that can include questions about your income and employment, all investments, savings and stocks, any retirement benefits including pensions and 401(k)s, along with everything about your home, any other real estate along with personal property, art, and any special collections, just to provide a few examples.

If there is a business, there will be a series of interrogatories about that as well as your lifestyle and expenses. Questions can also delve into the reason for the breakdown of the marriage and the divorce as well as a request for a list of witnesses who will be called if your divorce goes to trial. Custody and health issues are among other topics that may also be included in the questions.

In some cases, interrogatories are simple and consist of several questions over a few pages. In more complicated divorces, interrogatories can include hundreds of questions over many pages. They must be answered under oath and usually require that, along with the answers, documents such as verification of income, bank statements, credit card statements, tax returns, and the like be supplied.

Interrogatories may sometimes also address health and child custody issues. Attorneys are involved with this and these interrogatories can become quite complicated.

SUBPOENAS

In many divorces where there are issues that go beyond the scope of interrogatories, attorneys may issue subpoenas. These are legal documents that go to a third party such as a bank, credit card company, phone service provider, and other businesses or entities where records may be relevant to your divorce. The purpose is to get backup information as you build your case.

In my cases where gambling is an issue, I may subpoena local casinos for gambling records. There can be situations in which a spouse is accused of abusing credit cards; some of my clients' wives have been addicted to online shopping, and those records can be subpoenaed. In cases where allegations of an extramarital affair are made, obtaining credit card statements or hotel or motel records can be invaluable. Pornography is a frequent issue and many people now use credit cards to access X-rated sites, providing a paper trail.

When someone is not being fully candid in answers to interrogatories or trying to hide assets or debts, subpoenas can be extremely helpful. I have had cases where someone failed to disclose a bank or credit card account. Sometimes money disappears and a well-placed subpoena can help shake it to the surface.

DEPOSITIONS

In divorces where the marital estate is substantial or where there are a lot of suspicions as to hidden assets or a double life, a deposition can be an important tool. I have had cases where someone has absconded with hundreds of thousands of dollars, or took money and claimed to have lost it in Las Vegas. I've seen situations where there might be a new business that is not disclosed or a business that has been transferred into someone else's name. These are just a few of many examples where a deposition can be invaluable.

A deposition is a statement under oath taken with a court reporter present to transcribe or record every statement made by the person being deposed and the attorneys, word for word. Depositions are admissible in court and can be valuable if a case actually goes to trial because statements during the deposition can be used for cross-examination in the event of a trial. I have used depositions to find out what my client's husband or wife will be like in a formal courtroom setting. How credible will he or she be if the case goes to trial?

In addition, a deposition can be taken of any witnesses who may be important in helping to achieve a divorce settlement or to help you prepare for trial. Depositions are now being taken by video and even Skype when a witness is out of state and can't be present for the deposition. Courts also allow out-of-state witnesses to testify by phone in certain situations as well.

I urge my clients to be truthful in depositions and in court. Still, people lie all of the time. And once you lie in court or in a deposition, even if it is a minor detail, your credibility is shot for anything else going forward in your case. I have seen someone lie over a small detail – maybe involving the children being present with a girlfriend or over a problem with medications, for example. From then on, the judge will not believe anything they say. Lies come back to haunt you.

DIGITAL DISCOVERY

Now that we are in the age of social media and digital communication, we have a whole new world for discovery. Pictures or messages on Facebook, YouTube, and Twitter, for example, are all discoverable in a divorce. A husband's picture with another woman or a wife's Facebook post about an outing with her children and boyfriend can come back to haunt in a divorce.

In one case, my client's husband posted a picture of his girlfriend and three children giving the finger to his wife on the Internet, also texting it to his wife.

In another situation a misplaced email led my client to discover that her husband was looking to meet men on gay sites. Until then, she didn't know he was gay and living a double life.

In some situations, inflammatory emails in custody cases cost parents custody of their children. People push send on their phones and computers without thinking, posting so much damaging information that phones and computers have become treasure troves for divorce attorneys.

Cellphones can be ordered to be produced as evidence. Smartphones are minicomputers. Text messages can be subpoenaed. The former mayor of

Detroit was brought down by his text messages disclosing an affair with one of his key assistants — a relationship he lied about in a trial.

Computers can be taken and analyzed by experts. Even when you push the delete key on your computer, an imprint remains and can be retrieved. Email can be fair game, too. There are companies that will go through and analyze your computer or smartphones.

In fact, technology is far ahead of the law. I recently handled a divorce during which I learned from a client that if you have an iPhone with a family account, you can not only download and follow email messages from your spouse's phone, but you can also track the whereabouts of your spouse through an app.

Of course, the dangers here are that false information can be planted and pictures can be Photoshopped. It is important to be able to trace the source of messages, documents, and photos — issues an attorney can help with as you go through your divorce.

Also, bugs can be planted in your computer. Tracking devices like LoJack can be planted on your car. Your house can be bugged. Be aware and be paranoid.

I have lectured on this topic in national webinars. The technological devices are endless. I've seen email intercepted, computers hacked, phones tapped, and video devices placed in homes.

A lot of this is now illegal, but the technology is far outpacing the law. There are criminal statutes covering phone tapping, tracking devices on cars, keystroke devices on computers, and placing bugs or video recording devices throughout the home. I have had cases where emails to my client were being intercepted by her husband and then shared with his attorney. This is a violation of the law and could result in criminal charges against not only the husband, but also possibly the attorney if he or she is a party to this illegal activity. It is important to talk to your attorney, as the laws differ from state to state.

Another issue in discovery is when a business has two sets of books. I have had cases involving restaurants, small grocery stores, liquor stores, gas stations, and certain professional practices where cash was king. Beauty and nail salons, personal trainers, exotic dancers, and gentlemen's clubs have been factors in some of the divorces I've dealt with over the years, and figuring out the values and amounts of real income is challenging, to say the least.

In cases where reported income is low, but there's a lot of cash, we might have accountants do a lifestyle analysis to demonstrate that the tax returns are just the tip of the iceberg.

And forensic accountants can be hired to assist with discovery and the valuation of a business or professional practice. These can be very time-consuming and expensive procedures — but critical, when many thousands and even millions of dollars are at stake.

Every case is different.

Just remember that discovery is the foundation for a proper resolution. It's the way to be sure that when it comes to your divorce, you are playing with a full deck.

Wrapping Up

It's important that you receive all you are entitled to in your divorce. Affidavits, interrogatories, subpoenas, depositions, and other forms of discovery help put together the pieces of your marital puzzle. This is to protect you as your divorce moves forward to its ultimate resolution.

Notes

CHAPTER SIXTEEN

Property & Debt

1
2
3
4
5
6
7
8
9
10
11
12
13
14
15
16
17
18
19
20
21

Divorce is a balancing act. The laws differ from state to state regarding division of property and debt, and every situation is different.

Most states are equitable distribution status, which means that a fair and equitable distribution of property — not necessarily 50-50 — is the goal. In community property states, most assets acquired during the course of the marriage are divided equally between the parties. Your attorney will be able to explain how this works in the state where you live.

Think of a game of *Monopoly*. If you want Park Place and Boardwalk, you will have to give up something to get it. It's a matter of trading items back and forth to achieve a result that makes sense.

There are different types of property and debts, and they don't all come into play in every divorce.

REAL ESTATE

Real property can include several types.

First and foremost comes the marital home. In many divorces, it's the major asset. After the real estate crash in 2008, many people lost their homes, or if they didn't, came through it to find they were underwater because the amount due on their mortgage was greater than the value of the home.

The economy has been improving and with it, home values. Recently, when the marital home was being sold as part of the divorce settlement, I've had several cases where the home has sold within hours after being placed on the market — some with bidding wars and offers over the original asking price.

It's common in divorce for both the husband and wife to want the home. It used to be common for the parent who would have custody of the minor children to obtain the right to stay in the house for a number of years — until the youngest child reached the age of majority and graduated high school or until there was a remarriage, for example. These situations called for a sale of the home at a future date or a buyout based on future value and equity. Today, with more parties having shared custodial arrangements, this rarely happens. Instead, the house will typically be sold or one party immediately buys the other out.

When the house is underwater, usually one party will keep it and try to refinance once there is positive equity again. In some cases, I have advised clients to do a short sale where the bank will agree to take less than the mortgage balance due if the home is sold. In others, my clients have had to bring a check to closing to cover negative equity in the home after the closing costs and real estate commissions are taken into account. Again, this is changing as the economy improves.

Typically, women become emotionally attached to the family home more than men. But I generally advise my clients not to become too enamored with it. While change is difficult, in many situations it is better not to keep the home. Many — especially older ones — are money pits. What if you need a new roof or a new furnace, have leaks, or discover black mold? The list can be endless.

I often tell my clients that it makes sense to start fresh after a divorce and not take over the responsibilities — and too often, the burden — of keeping your home. In addition, as you move on in life, a new significant other or spouse will not want to reside where your first spouse did. Often there are too many bad memories.

The key is that every situation is different. When it comes to your home, what makes sense for your best friend, neighbor, or relative may make no sense for you.

Other real estate can include vacation homes, rental and other investment property, vacant lots, and commercial real estate including a building where a family business is located.

Many people also own timeshares. They are usually a bad investment; I have rarely seen a timeshare that appreciates in value and they are also very difficult to sell. In that event, couples often end up sharing or rotating the use of timeshares after the divorce.

BUSINESS INTERESTS

I have been involved with hundreds of divorces where there was some type of business entity involved. These have run the gamut, from fast food franchises, bars, and restaurants to liquor stores, gas stations, car washes, dry cleaners, cemetery lot sales, funeral homes, nightclubs, gentlemen's clubs, car dealerships, jewelry stores, law practices, medical practices, accounting practices, veterinary practices, building contractors, and real estate development companies, to name a few. Value can run from under $100,000 to millions.

Some are owned by the husband and wife together, and trying to come up with a value that everyone can agree on so one can buy the other out can be impossible. Though they can't remain in a marriage, some couples choose to stay together in business. Such was the case in several divorces I handled recently involving a pizza franchise, dental practice, and accounting firm.

It is important to bear in mind that every situation is different and what works for one couple will be impossible for the next. If you and your spouse agree to remain in business together, you can draw up an agreement as to what do to in the future but you do not have to place an immediate value on the business.

On the other hand, if you are going to go your separate ways completely then the business or professional practice will have to be valued. In these situations, attorneys bring in experts such as forensic accountants who specialize in putting a value on your business or practice. In some areas, such as with dental practices that are bought and sold frequently, sometimes brokers who buy and sell dental practices are brought in to assess value. While they can be complicated, these valuations are important in any divorce where there is a business, or to evaluate such factors as a professional degree or license, or liquor licenses, which also can have value.

In one recent case the husband was part owner of a gentlemen's club. To say the least, it was a cash business. The dancers pay for the right to dance and the bartender, waitresses, and parking attendants also pay to work in exchange for tips, which can be substantial. The owners make money from liquor and food sales, as well as the payments from all of the people working there. The value and income streams can be in the millions of dollars, much of it not reported.

Another recent case involved a construction company. There were millions of dollars at stake and the experts were millions of dollars apart on estimating value. Here, a good mediator helped negotiate a compromise on the value to open the way to a settlement.

I have had cases involving restaurants where there were duplicate books. Coming up with valuations was extremely problematic.

In professional practices, we often look at the cash flow, income streams, and the value of any equipment and patient lists, when applicable.

It's common to see a small business or professional practice decline somewhat at this time, with a corresponding decrease in income. Why? Sometimes it is the economy. More often, though, it's because the person who wants to keep the business tries to minimize the value as the spouse who is being bought out tries to maximize value. Other times, it's because of the psychological stress of a divorce; people are not functioning as well as they normally would. I see these situations frequently.

PERSONAL PROPERTY

This is a broad category. Following are some examples, though this list is not exhaustive.

- Savings and checking accounts
- Stock brokerage accounts
- Stock options that can be a benefit of employment
- Any other investments
- Etrade accounts

- Gold, silver, and precious gems
- Bonds
- Collections

One person's junk is another client's treasure. While some collections have very little value, others can be worth millions.

Collections can include sports memorabilia, cars, books including first edition and classics, stamps, coins, ceramic figurines, china, art, wines, model cars, antiques, guns, comic books, magazines (one client had a *Playboy* collection), autographs, jewelry, watches, and other items of value.

In some situations, we arrive at a division of personal property by trading back and forth between the spouses. In others, we bring in appraisers.

Early in my career, I was involved in a divorce where my client had a 300 SL Gull Wing 1959 Mercedes, which was listed among the assets and today might be worth more than a half-million dollars. The wife's attorney never asked about it and no one tried to value it. When in doubt as to the value of an object or collection, have it appraised.

I recently settled a case where the clients were involved in a gold and jewelry business. They had thousands of precious gems that had been removed from their settings, with a total value that could have been more than $1 million. We brought in appraisers for some of the jewels and the clients also tried to sell the stones by creating a special website and splitting the proceeds from sales. Unique situations call for creative solutions.

Jewelry that was a gift – engagement or wedding rings, for example – are not subject to division. The person who receives the gift is normally allowed to keep it. On the other hand, a lot of jewelry purchased as an investment would be subject to division as part of the divorce settlement.

Other assets that I have dealt with include cars, boats, yachts, planes, and toys including motorcycles, all-terrain vehicles, Jet Skis, snowmobiles, vacation and motor homes, and even golf carts.

An important factor in many divorces is your retirement accounts and those of your spouse. Retirement accounts are built with pre-tax assets, while most other items of personal property are based on after tax value. When we divide pre- and after-tax assets, it is important to remember that there can be tax implications and value differences. You can't mix apples and oranges.

Retirement assets include 401(k)s, IRAs, 403(b)s, and other plans. Some pensions pay out a certain sum of money in the future based on your age and years of service. These can include a teacher's or union pension, by way of example. These are all factors that must be weighed.

DIVISION OF DEBT

After listing and considering your assets, the next issue is to take stock of debt. In some cases, there isn't enough money to go around and bankruptcy has to be considered. In recent years, I have had couples who had to consider bankruptcy along with their divorce and I would coordinate both with a bankruptcy attorney. An improving economy has meant fewer bankruptcies. Still, many couples live over their heads and when a divorce happens, they can't even afford their reduced lifestyle, let alone overwhelming debts.

In many divorces, credit cards are an issue. When one spouse is out of control in his or her spending, this will be an issue in the division of assets and liabilities. During the divorce, it is essential to get control over spending and see exactly what is going on.

In these credit card battles, sometimes one spouse will take over more of the responsibility for paying the debts. Sometimes they will be paid by liquidating other assets. Charges incurred right before or during a divorce are often carefully scrutinized to make sure that they are not frivolous or unusual. I have had several cases where a wife had plastic surgery and even breast augmentation right before a divorce was filed. Who should pay for that? Husbands will say that if they can't receive any of the benefits, why should they pay the bill?

That new fur coat or jewelry can be an issue as well. It's the same with an expensive vacation right before a divorce. I have had many battles over such purchases or debts that were incurred right before the filing of a divorce.

Other property issues include gifts or inherited property, lottery winnings, and settlements from an auto accident, medical malpractice case, worker's compensation claim or other injury claim.

There can be Social Security claims as well. I have dealt with issues involving royalties from songs, patents, copyrights, and book sales. All of these issues must be dealt with as part of your divorce.

I often tell clients that a divorce is like a Rubik's Cube. Until all of the parts are fully in alignment, there is no settlement. Property division is important but it is not the only piece of the puzzle, especially if you have minor children.

Wrapping Up

Identifying what you have and what you owe as well as how to divide the allocation of these various items is an essential part of divorce. Every case is different, and creativity can resolve even the most difficult financial issues in your divorce.

Notes

CHAPTER SEVENTEEN

About The Pets

When it comes to divorce and custody, it isn't always only about the kids. People love their dogs, cats, and other pets, too. Pets can be an emotional issue and they've come up in plenty of the divorces I've handled.

Laws differ from state to state. In Michigan, pets are considered to be property. The law might allow for the judgment to include payment of vet bills for a dog or cats, but it stops short of pet visitation or custody, for example.

However, pets represent a multibillion-dollar industry. More and more courts are looking at them as more than just an object to be divided.

Many couples try to schedule some type of shared custodial arrangements or visitation for their dogs or cats. I've seen people fight over a bird, and I've dealt with cases involving pygmy pigs.

I recently settled a divorce involving a horse farm, and the horses were part of the judgment. In another, the divorce was triggered by the wife's decision to have the three family dogs put to sleep without consulting her husband. She claimed they might be rabid because they had just cornered and killed a raccoon, but never asked her husband or called a vet before deciding to terminate their lives.

There have been times that I've included clauses in a divorce judgment addressing pets, only to have them eliminated by the judge. One judge even stated on the record, "I don't do pets!"

What do you do? Try to work these issues out. If you live in a state that recognizes pets can be a factor in a divorce settlement, then some formal arrangement can be worked out. If not, perhaps a side agreement that is not part of the divorce judgment can be arranged.

Perhaps the pets can go back and forth along with your children, if you have them. Or maybe you will have to divide your pets as you would any other personal property.

This is an area of the law that is evolving. If you have a dog, cat, or other beloved pet, and if their handling is an issue, talk to your attorney about how laws and rules apply in the event of a divorce.

Wrapping Up

Pets may be part of the family, but in many states, they are considered property. Talk to your attorney about the options if you and your spouse can't agree about where your dog will sit or stay.

Notes

CHAPTER EIGHTEEN

Domestic Violence

I wish that domestic violence issues did not go hand in hand with divorce. Sadly, they often do. Early in my career when I was just starting to build my practice as a divorce attorney, one of my clients was a victim of spouse abuse. During the divorce, her husband called me and said that he wished that he had beaten that f—— b— more so that she could not have crawled into my office to retain me. This was several decades ago, when domestic violence was not recognized to the extent that it is today.

Fast forward to a situation that happened recently. A divorce was finalized in the community where I live. The settlement agreement had a clause requiring the husband to vacate the marital home on a given date. The night before the deadline, he began shooting and the police were called. An officer was killed and after a 15-hour standoff, the man was found in the bedroom, surrounded by guns, dead from a self-inflicted gunshot. This hit home all the more because it was three houses away from where my grandchildren reside.

Police officers and sheriff's deputies universally say that domestic disputes are among the most volatile – and often, deadly – situations they deal with. I have had clients murdered during a divorce. One was seriously injured and disfigured after her former husband stabbed her multiple times. There have been suicides during and after a divorce; I can't say that divorce caused the suicide, but it could very well have contributed to or been the straw that broke the camel's back.

Our headlines and newscasts are filled with the latest horror story of domestic violence where a deranged spouse will kill not only a husband or wife during or after a divorce, but also the children.

We live in an age where there is too much violence. Emotions churn out of control. In every marriage, there is a fine line between love and hate.

Domestic violence is widespread, crossing all socioeconomic classes. As many as one-third of our nation's families experience domestic violence. Some studies have indicated that two-thirds of all marriages have been touched by physical or emotional abuse. I have seen it in every religion and ethnic and cultural background. In many families, it is a well-kept secret.

MANY FORMS OF ABUSE

As I write this chapter, I have been retained by a woman with a history of emotional abuse in her marriage who parted ways with her original attorney. Her previous attorney told her that emotional abuse does not count. Quite frankly, emotional mistreatment can scar as badly as physical abuse. It does count, but sadly, it is often much more difficult to prove. Medical records describing physical wounds or photos showing evidence of abuse are much easier to demonstrate in a trial or hearing than evidence of a long history of psychological or emotional battering.

While abuse is predominantly a crime against women, I have represented both men and women who were victims of domestic violence: physical, psychological, or verbal.

Thankfully, our courts are now much more cognizant of these issues. There are networks of shelters for victims of abuse throughout the United States, and I have been involved with many shelters for victims of domestic violence over the years. In addition, law enforcement and the courts recognize the need for personal protection orders or other legal remedies to provide some protection for victims of abuse.

Still, an injunction or personal protection order can only go so far. Tragically, there are too many instances in which a spouse makes a deliberate decision to kill or injure family members, despite protection from the courts.

And criminal statutes to protect victims are not always used or enforced. Divorces with domestic violence, especially where the abuse is psychological and verbal, can be challenging to say the least.

Some of my clients have refused to leave an abusive situation because they believe that staying is the safest thing to do. Many victims are too frightened to file papers, contact the police, or otherwise become involved with the legal system. Clients have told me how they lied when police were called in response to an abusive situation, or would say that they had fallen when they went to the hospital or for other medical treatment, rather than tell the truth about being struck or pushed.

Social media and the Internet have also become factors in domestic abuse. Very often in recent years, one spouse or the other posts derogatory or demeaning pictures or hurtful statements on Facebook, YouTube, or other sites.

Revenge porn is a relatively new term describing the placement of compromising photos of a former spouse or partner on specific websites. I have had cases where nude photos have been posted. Recently, a woman lost custody of her children partly because she was posting demeaning and inflammatory statements about her husband on Facebook for the whole world to see.

At the end of this chapter is a Power and Control Wheel, which I often show to clients. It is amazing how many have a spouse who fits the profile covered in this wheel.

POINTS TO PONDER

Here are some pointers for a spouse going through a divorce from someone who may be abusive – important for both the abuser and victim to consider.

If you are concerned about being abusive to your partner or spouse, ask yourself these questions. If your answers are in the affirmative, consider them to be warning signs of a problem.

Was there violence in your family?

During conflict, do you often threaten someone, break things, punch walls, slam doors, ignore your spouse, or leave?

Do you have mood swings where one moment you feel loving and affectionate, and the next angry and threatening?

Have you ever shoved, grabbed, hit, slapped, or choked your spouse, or any past partners or former spouses?

Do you find it difficult to talk to your spouse about your feelings, hopes, and fears?

Do you tend to blame others for your behavior – especially your spouse?

Are you a very jealous person?

Do you try to control how your spouse thinks and/or dresses, who your spouse sees, how your spouse spends time, how your spouse spends money?

Do you try to discourage your spouse from seeing friends or family?

Do your conversations quickly escalate into threats of separation or divorce?

Do you threaten to hurt your spouse, yourself, or others if your spouse talks about leaving you?

Do you do or say things that are designed to make your partner feel crazy or stupid?

Do you blame alcohol, drugs, stress, or other life events for your behavior?

Do you feel guilty after aggressive behavior or strive for your spouse's forgiveness?

Do you think you could never live without your spouse, yet other times you want your spouse out?

Do you use sex, money, or other favors as a way to "make up" after conflict?

Is your spouse afraid of you sometimes?

Are you living with a spouse who is a potential abuser? There are often indications that your spouse/partner is a potential abuser. Here are some warning signs that you may be the victim of abuse.

Did your spouse grow up in a violent family? People who grew up in a family where their parent was beaten or where their siblings were abused are more likely to become abusers.

Does your spouse avoid confrontations with people who could fight back, and take it out on you instead?

Does your spouse overreact to small problems or frustrations such as not finding a parking space or having to wait in line? I have seen many divorces where road rage or other situations would then trigger domestic violence by a spouse.

Is your spouse destructive when angry? Does your partner punch walls or throw things when upset? Does your spouse smash dishes or break valuables in a rage? Does your spouse drive like a maniac just to scare you?

Is your spouse cruel to animals? People who abuse animals are often abusive to their spouses and children.

Does your spouse abuse alcohol or other drugs, blaming them for inappropriate behavior? Alcohol or drug use is present in domestic violence situations about half the time.

Is your spouse very insecure, or worried about sexual attractiveness or performance? Does your spouse boast about sexual ability and success with members of the opposite sex?

Does your spouse think that everyone treats him or her badly? Does he or she talk about "getting even" or "getting back" at people?

Has your partner hit former partners, spouses, or significant others? A person who has battered before will batter again.

Is your spouse extremely jealous and possessive? Does your spouse want you to be with him/her all the time, even when it is inconvenient for you? Does your spouse demand a minute-by-minute accounting of your time, or accuse you of having affairs? Does your spouse use his or her jealousy or concern for your safety to limit your activities?

Does your spouse discourage or prevent you from going to school, getting a job, working for a promotion, or doing other things that can make you more independent? I have handled many divorces where my client has been denied her right to finish school, get a job, or even to remain in a high-paying career.

Does your spouse drive your friends and family away or put a wedge between you and them? Does your partner criticize others for "putting ideas" into your head?

Does your spouse have rigid traditional ideas about what men and women should be and act like? Does your spouse treat you like personal property, expecting you to anticipate his or her needs? If your spouse is male, does he feel that men are in charge of disciplining their wives and children? Does your spouse make all of the decisions for both of you? Is your spouse secretive and will he or she keep information from you?

If your spouse is male, does he treat women like second-class citizens? Does he dislike women, except for sexual purposes? Does he talk about women as if they are good only for sex? Does he tell misogynistic jokes and expect you to laugh? Does he make fun of strong, independent women?

Does your spouse play with or seem obsessed with weapons, or threaten to use them? *Has* your spouse used them?

If your spouse is male, does he read or view pornography? The Internet has been revolutionary in making pornographic materials available. Does he try to persuade or force you to act out what he reads or sees?

Does your spouse go through extreme mood swings?

When your spouse gets angry, are you afraid? Do you try to anticipate what your spouse wants to avoid angry confrontations? Do you change your behavior to avoid upsetting him or her? Do you feel like you are walking on eggshells?

If your spouse is male, does he force you to have sex or do things you don't want to? Does he call you sexually derogatory names? Does he try to force you to get drunk or high, then do things he knows you do not want to? Forced sex is rape, even in a marriage or if the person is your partner or boyfriend.

Does your spouse take your money from you? Does your spouse make you ask for money?

Does your spouse threaten to hurt or kill you, your children, family, or friends?

Does your spouse threaten suicide if you leave?

Are you afraid to leave or break up with your spouse?

Has your spouse hit you? Choked or bitten you? Locked or tied you up?

No person deserves to suffer violence at the hands of an abuser. If you recognize your spouse and/or yourself in these questions, tell your attorney! Don't wait for your spouse to magically change. It won't happen. Get help. There are many resources available. (*See the list at right.*)

I have represented so many spouses who are rescuers and believed that they could change an abuser. They are victims, and the only way to change the situation is for the

Need Help?

Battered Women's Justice Project
800-903-0111 Ext. 1
bwjp. org

Family Violence Prevention Fund
415-252-8900

Futures Without Violence
415-678-5500
futureswithoutviolence.org

Legal Resource Center on Violence Against Women
800-556-4053
lrcvaw.org

National Center on Protection Orders and Full Faith and Credit
800-903-0111
fullfaithandcredit.org

National Clearinghouse for the Defense of Battered Women
800-903-0111 Ext. 3
ncdbw.org

National Coalition Against Domestic Violence
303-839-1852
ncadv.org

National Domestic Violence Hotline
800-799-SAFE (7233)
thehotline.org

Rape, Abuse & Incest National Network
800-656-HOPE (4673)
rainn.org

Safe Horizons
212-227-3000
victimservices.org

Stalking Resource Center of the National Center for Victims of Crime
202-467-8700
victimsofcrime.org

Power & Control Wheel

PHYSICAL VIOLENCE

SEXUAL VIOLENCE

Power & Control

Using Coercion and Threats
- Threats are statements that promise negative consequences for certain behaviors or actions. For example, "I'll kill you if you ever leave me."
- Coercion is a statement or action that implies, indirectly, negative or positive consequences for certain behaviors or actions. For example, cleaning the house and buying flowers the day after abuse.

Using Intimidation
- Making her afraid by using looks, actions, gestures, intoxication, "silent treatment." • Smashing things. • Destroying property. • Harming pets. • Displaying weapons. • Yelling. • Stalking her. • Slamming doors. • Driving recklessly. • Acting "crazy," invincible, or like "I have nothing to lose."

Using Economic Abuse
- Concealing or denying information about finances.
- Using family/her assets without her knowledge or permission.
- Preventing her from getting, keeping or leaving a job. • Damaging her credit rating.
- Making her ask for money. • Destroying checkbooks, credit cards, money, or property.
- Giving her an allowance.

Using Emotional Abuse
- Putting her down.
- Making her feel bad about herself. • Calling her names.
- Making her think she's crazy.
- Playing mind games • Humiliating her.
- Making her feel guilty. • Using things that matter to her against her. • Negatively comparing her to others. • Unreasonable demands or expectations.
- Honeymooning her. • Perfectionism.

Using Male Privilege
- Defining what men's and women's roles are.
- Defining what is and isn't "important." • Controlling the decision-making process. • Making and enforcing self-serving rules. • Treating her as an inferior. • Acting like the "master of the castle." • Believing or saying, "it's my right as a man to behave this way."
- Acting like God.

Using Isolation
- Controlling her access to resources such as birth control, reproductive choices, medical attention, money, education, employment opportunities, family/friends, transportation, phone use.
- Using jealousy to justify actions.
- Embarrassing her in front of others.
- Kidnapping her. • Convincing her that seeing her family or friends is "harmful to our relationship."

Using Others
- Using the children to relay messages.
- Using visitation to harass her. • Threatening to take the children away.
- Using custody of the children as leverage. • Abusing the children.
- Sexual abuse of the children. • Kidnapping the children. • Degrading her about her relationships. • Using her job, family, friends, religion, etc. as leverage.

Using Obfuscation
- Denying or minimizing the existence, severity, or impact of abusive behavior • Blaming or otherwise shifting responsibility for abusive behavior. • Lying about, concealing, withholding, or omitting information, situations, or behavior to gain advantage.
- Pretending to be a victim to gain sympathy, support, or allies.
- Using intoxication as an excuse.

Originally created by the Domestic Abuse Intervention Project, Duluth, Minnesota; revised by and copied courtesy of the Alternatives to Domestic Aggression Program, Catholic Social Services of Washtenaw County, Ann Arbor, Michigan.

abusive spouse to get help. You cannot fix someone who refuses to seek help or denies that there is a problem. Tragically, in some marriages the end is not divorce, but serious injury or death.

FALSE CHARGES

Last but not least, I have had many cases where there have been false accusations of domestic violence made by a spouse against the other one. Sometimes this is a ploy in a custody case.

Get your attorney involved at once. Don't wait. Timing can be critical. I have had clients who have ignored police calls and reports with serious legal consequences.

I wish to thank Beth Morrison, executive director of The Haven, for her feedback and assistance with this chapter.

Wrapping Up

The signs of domestic violence are clear. There are steps victims in an abusive marriage can take to protect themselves personally and legally. A good divorce attorney will be empathetic, knowledgeable, and proactive to help you deal with these traumatic and critical issues as part of your divorce.

Notes

Notes

_____

_____

_____

_____

_____

_____

_____

_____

_____

_____

_____

_____

_____

_____

_____

_____

_____

_____

_____

_____

_____

_____

_____

CHAPTER NINETEEN

Here Comes The Judge

Practicing family law for more than 40 years, I have appeared before many judges. In fact, when I first started my career as a lawyer, I clerked for some circuit court judges in Detroit who handled all types of cases, including divorce. It gave me an inside view of the courts — and judges — at the inception of my legal career.

Over the years I have seen many wonderful judges, as well as some who should never be on the bench. I have appeared before some judges who would make wonderful rulings in the morning, but would be a different person in the afternoon. Having one drink too many at lunch can change a personality, especially when the judge is an alcoholic.

I have appeared before some judges who didn't show up for court or would be hours late while their courtroom was filled with attorneys and clients just sitting there waiting and wondering why their cases weren't getting heard.

A well-known judge in one of the counties where I practice was opposed to divorce. Then he got a divorce himself and it turned out that he lived a double life with two wives — one legal and one not — and two sets of children. It shows that judges are human and have the same frailties as other human beings.

The difference is that judges have tremendous power. They make the most important decisions affecting the lives of anyone going through a divorce. They have the last word on your economic future — whether you will receive alimony and how much, as well as how your property is divided. They can decide where you will live and how much time your children will spend with you and your spouse. The personality, beliefs, and bias your judge brings, as well as his or her life experiences, can definitely play a role in judicial decisions.

Yet, you have no control over how your judge is selected. Where I practice family law, judges are assigned at random by blind draw and you can't choose or change your judge. If you are unhappy with the judge assigned to your case, it is extremely difficult to get it changed. Laws and customs regarding judge assignments can vary from state to state. This is an issue that you should discuss with your attorney.

This is what I believe makes a good family law judge.
1. Your judge should listen to the arguments of your attorneys and show compassion. I have seen many judges cut off arguments or who don't even seem to be listening to what is going on as a case is being argued.

2. Your judge should not lose control of his or her courtroom, or in the courtroom. I have seen judges lose their temper and stalk off the bench, or even throw a tantrum in court. This can be a chilling and frightening experience.

3. Your judge should not let attorneys argue and ramble on endlessly. Everyone should have a chance to speak, but it should be handled with decorum and not endless attacks by one attorney against the other. Your judge should also know when to cut arguments off in court.

4. Your judge should be fair and evenhanded. Putting aside his or her worldview, the judge should try to dispense justice with understanding and compassion.

5. You want your judge to be decisive. One of the most frustrating things for attorneys and clients is to go to court and then after arguing your case, have the judge take the matter under advisement and fail to make a ruling. It is so important to have finality in a divorce. You want rulings made on the issues in your case so that you can go on with your life. Even if you disagree — and no one agrees with everything in a divorce — you will find that a decision, maybe not perfect or completely favorable to you, is almost always better than no decision. Life in limbo can be excruciating.

6. Your judge should be on time. When court is set for 8:30 or 9 a.m., it should start at close to those times. Now, court is just one part of a judge's duties. He or she may be dealing with phone calls or meeting with attorneys in chambers, so sometimes there will be delays. But sitting around waiting for your case to start is costly — emotionally and economically. A good judge knows that and will try to be on time.

7. Some judges refuse to talk to attorneys in chambers about your case. Good judges will meet with attorneys — and sometimes even the parties to a divorce — in chambers. I feel very strongly that a meeting with attorneys through a pretrial or settlement conference, providing the judge with the opportunity to listen to some of the key issues, often helps to settle a case. Some judges will indicate their views about an issue, but suggest that they are open to testimony or evidence that could lead them to change their position. This is a way of sending a signal to the attorneys and parties, but also makes it clear that your judge is prepared to listen to all of the witnesses or facts should your case go to trial.

On this note, I believe that a good judge will set up meetings, even on the day of trial, to attempt to settle your case rather than just say, "If you can't settle, then call your first witness." Good judges recognize that trials are expensive, both financially and emotionally. Once you start saying things in open court to and about your soon-to-be former spouse, you create more wounds and it becomes more difficult for each of you to heal and move on with your lives. Trials should be a last resort, and a good judge knows this.

8. A good judge knows that he or she is a stranger to you and your spouse. A couple acting in a rational and constructive manner can make better decisions about their lives and those of their children than a stranger in a black robe can — and a good judge realizes that.

9. While a judge should always be in control of his or her courtroom and cases, you don't want a judge who is punitive or refuses to allow you and others going through a divorce to have your day in court. The old saying, "Justice delayed is justice denied," is so true. If your case is set for trial and is constantly being adjourned because of court docket conflicts or similar reasons, it is not helpful to you or your spouse. Of course, reasonable adjournments should be granted; some divorces take more time than others because of the complexities of a particular divorce or because the parties need more time psychologically before they can move on. But unlimited adjournments and delays are inexcusable.

10. I have found over the years that many cases can be settled after a trial has started. If your judge will start the trial and listen to you and your spouse and at least allow some evidence to be presented, this can often permit you to get some of your emotions and feelings off your chest. It gives you some empowerment and allows you to know that you are being listened to. This can often lead to a settlement in the middle of a trial without the need to complete the case.

    Some judges will give both spouses a chance to speak in an informal manner and then try to settle the case. This can work. For example, I tried a high-conflict divorce where there were many intertwined monetary, psychological, and criminal issues. After two days of testimony, the attorneys and clients talked in the courthouse cafeteria and settled without the need to complete the trial.

11. I believe that a good judge should show you and your attorney respect. In turn, your judge should also be respected. Don't lose sight of the fact that the judge has the power to decide your fate and that of your children.

12. We are not all alike. People from different cultural and ethnic

backgrounds think and react differently during a divorce. A good judge knows that and is sensitive to religious, ethnic, racial, and cultural differences. By recognizing and demonstrating understanding of cultural differences in a respectful way in court, a resolution to issues in a divorce can be achieved that might otherwise not have worked. In the area where I practice, there are people from all over the world. A cookie-cutter approach won't work. Your judge should recognize this.

13. When making a ruling, you want your judge to be clear and concise – to explain what he or she is doing and why. Too many times, my client, his or her spouse, and the other attorney walk out of court totally confused by a judge's ruling. I have seen too many cases where a judge wasn't listening, didn't understand the facts, or would make a ruling that made no sense at all. Clearly this helps no one.

14. Again, let me reiterate the fact that a good lawyer and a good judge understand that a trial should be a last resort after all other means of resolving a case have failed.

WHAT IS YOUR ROLE?

Let's now discuss what judges want from attorneys and clients. These are some do's and don'ts for court appearances that are based upon many years of appearing before hundreds of judges in thousands of divorces as well as in talking to judges and attorneys.

1. **Be prepared.** You and your attorney must communicate and discuss all issues in advance of a court appearance. It is critical that you understand what may or may not happen in court and what the possible consequences are. You and your attorney should be prepared to address all of the key issues of your divorce that may be raised in court, including motions, hearings, and trials.

2. **Brevity is important.** You and your attorney should be succinct. Some lawyers believe that you can overpower the other side by going on and on until everyone is exhausted. While some judges may be swayed by this, a much better approach is to be brief and to the point. If you can get your point across in five or 10 minutes, do it. Judges want to know what you want and why.

   If you have a written motion, most judges will have read it. Don't just repeat what is already in writing. Enhance it, add to it, bring up points to support your request for relief that were not covered in your written material, but don't go on endlessly. This can hurt your case in the long run.

3. **Dress appropriately.** I know that people dress in jeans more and more, but decorum and appropriate dress are important in court – as are first impressions. Male attorneys should be dressed in a suit and tie; females should be in suits, whether in skirt or pants.

Clients should dress well, too – if not in a dress or dress slacks or a suit and tie, at least in neat slacks and shirts. Shorts and jeans are never appropriate; you want to put your best foot forward and physical appearance and grooming are critical.

When I go to court, my goal is to win. That doesn't happen only through legal and oral presentations and demeanor, but is also based on how your attorney looks, how you look, and how you dress. In addition, do not chew gum in court or use a cellphone. Many courts also do not allow reading material in court except for your case pleadings.

4. **Make your own decisions.** While judges are paid to make decisions, most would prefer that you make the decisions about your lives and those of your children on your own. Judges have busy dockets with hundreds or thousands of cases each year. It is best for you to fly under the radar. If a judge gets to know you, it is usually for the wrong reasons – because you can't stop fighting, or go to court over every issue that arises.

If you are being unreasonable, or at least appear to be, it will not help your case.

5. **Be reasonable.** Don't ask for the sun and the moon. Attorneys who are unrealistic and appear to be greedy often lose. A good attorney will present the realities and advise you as to what is reasonable. This includes what to expect regarding your children and custody as well as economic issues.

6. **Remember that judges are human.** They have very busy dockets. They don't know you. Believe it or not, you can put the same set of facts before several different judges and get a different result with each one, which is terrifying.

In all issues of divorce and family law, we are dealing with a combination of fact-specific and legal issues. But every case is different and in family law, we deal with subtle shades of gray (usually not 50, though). There often are no absolutes or mathematical certainties, and the quality of justice can be very uneven.

All judges take their life experience to the bench. I have found that many women judges can be tougher on females than their male counterparts are. This is because they are working, often raising families, and in many cases, have gone through their own divorces. They believe that if they can earn a living, other women can as well. Personalities enter into the legal arena to a large degree.

7. **The five variables.** I tell my clients that there are at least five variables in every divorce. The first is who you are, your reasons for wanting to save or end your marriage, and your personality and emotional makeup. The second is your spouse, with the same factors that apply to you.

The third variable is your attorney. How experienced is he or she? What is his or her personality and approach to divorce? The fourth is your spouse's attorney and those same factors. The fifth is the judge.

Think about all of these variables carefully before deciding whether to go to trial. Remember that a trial is expensive both economically and emotionally. Don't let your attorney lead you into an unnecessary trial. Remember that this is about your life, that of your soon-to-be former spouse, and most importantly, the lives of your children.

Wrapping Up

A judge has a huge amount of influence over your divorce, especially if you go to trial or can't agree with your spouse on issues such as custody, visitation, and division of property, for example. It's important that you not only know how to act in court, but also what you have a right to expect from the judge overseeing your divorce.

Notes

Notes

CHAPTER TWENTY

Resolving Your Divorce

Over the years, I have seen many clients in denial over the fact that their marriage is ending – they can't comprehend or accept the fact that divorce is happening to them.

As we have discussed, everyone must go through the legal and emotional process. There are several ways to resolve a divorce.

JUST SIT DOWN

The first and easiest way to proceed is for a couple who have decided to end their marriage to sit down and discuss all of the issues. In these cases, there may be little left for an attorney to do but handle the filings.

Today, more and more people try to handle their divorce without a lawyer. The problem with that is there can be a lot of complicated and hard-to-understand issues and ins and outs. Even if you think that you know all of the answers, I urge anyone reading this book to at least talk to an attorney. It's important to know your legal rights before making final decisions on all of the issues that may or may not affect you in your divorce. This is not the time to be penny-wise and pound-foolish. Even with legal representation, a divorce does not have to be costly when everything is agreed to and there are no major issues.

TALKING IT OUT

Communication is critical. The next way to resolve a divorce is for a husband, wife, and their respective attorneys to get together and resolve all issues in one or more meetings.

I encourage my clients to talk. Some lawyers discourage that and I feel this is wrong. When the divorce is over, especially if you have children, you will have to figure out ways to communicate for the rest of your lives. On the other hand, if the relationship is abusive, then talking is often fruitless.

I had a case with millions of dollars involved in a long-term marriage where the children were all grown. Over a series of meetings with attorneys, the husband and wife, accountants, and financial planners, an entire settlement was worked out and put in writing – before the case was even filed. The parties avoided court and many thousands of dollars in attorney fees.

What is interesting about this case is that a number of years earlier, the same couple had filed for divorce and been involved in numerous court hearings with a great deal of acrimony as well as spending countless thousands of dollars on attorneys. They eventually reconciled for a while. This time, we were able to settle everything in advance, which was best for everyone.

COLLABORATIVE LAW

The next scenario is one that is developing in many states and is called collaborative practice – divorce with an eye to the future. Your marriage may be ending, but your family still goes on. I am trained in collaborative divorce law and have seen its benefits firsthand.

Here is how it works. The clients will seek out attorneys who are trained in the collaborative approach. The husband has his collaborative attorney and the wife hers. Some cases involve a mediator who is trained in collaborative law, as well as accountants or other financial experts. Where there are children, there can be a therapist or other person trained to assist with regard to custody and visitation/parenting time issues so they can be resolved in an amicable and nonconfrontational manner.

In the collaborative approach, the parties and their team enter into an agreement that they will meet and not file for divorce until a settlement of all issues is reached and in writing. If a settlement can't be reached, the penalty is that the attorneys, financial experts, and other team members must resign from the case. At that point, the couple is free to retain lawyers for traditional litigation. This is so important because it encourages all parties to stay out of court and resolve the issues.

Between meetings, there will be homework assignments given to everyone to narrow the issues, make sure that everything is fully disclosed and all issues are covered, and everyone's rights are fully protected.

Collaborative law is not for everyone. But it works. In one case, I represented the wife in a long-term marriage where there was one minor child. It took several meetings over a number of months, but we were able to resolve everything before the divorce was filed. This included complicated financial issues involving a professional practice, alimony, retirement accounts, and several homes.

If we had gone through traditional litigation, the clients would have spent many more thousands of dollars in attorney and expert fees, not to mention the emotional toll.

I have seen the collaborative approach work in numerous situations and feel that it is a great solution for people who are willing to work together with trained professionals to end their marriages in a civil and dignified manner without going through the extra thousands of dollars and trauma that a court battle entails. You do not want to lose control and have a stranger in a black robe decide the fates of you and your children. Collaborative law is a useful tool for tailoring a result that fits your family, and that is critical. In every collaborative case I have been involved in, the clients have been committed to the process and it has worked.

MEDIATION

Mediation is another way to stay out of court. I am also trained and certified as a mediator and believe strongly in the process.

There are several types of mediation. The first is when you and your spouse decide to go to a trained mediator as a couple. The mediator can be an attorney, therapist, or other person who is trained in mediation.

The mediator will meet with the couple and help them explore options as to how to resolve a divorce, typically all together in one room and with full disclosure of assets, liabilities, and issues. It takes good communication and a willingness to work together in an effort to end your marriage with as little acrimony as possible and with a goal of staying out of court and keeping your costs down.

Where I practice, mediation is very common as a requirement before you go to trial. In most divorces where there are issues that cannot be easily resolved without mediation, the judge will ask the attorneys to agree upon a mediator or will appoint one from a list of certified mediators.

The mediator then sets a date to meet with the attorneys and the parties to the divorce. In advance of the mediation session, each attorney prepares a mediation summary providing a history of the marriage, information about the husband and wife, age, health, length of the marriage, jobs, education, and income as well as a list of assets and liabilities. If there are children, custody, child support, visitation, and other child-related issues will be discussed as well.

Each attorney also prepares a list of what the spouses are seeking and why. When I am the attorney representing a husband or wife and we are going to mediation, I prepare a proposal that is reasonable. I have found that asking for too much reduces the chance of settling your divorce in mediation. Remember that pigs get slaughtered.

Of course, there must be room to negotiate and you never want to ask for what you expect to end up with or you will end up with a lot less than you hoped. Be in the same ballpark; a good mediator will be working with everyone to achieve a result that makes sense for you and your spouse — not for someone else.

A mediation session is held during which the attorneys, mediator, and husband and wife try to resolve the case. Some mediators will have everyone in the same conference room together. This works in certain situations, but I feel both as a mediator and as an attorney representing a client in a divorce mediation that it is better to be in separate rooms during this process. Why? In most mediations that I have been involved in, everything discussed while the parties are in separate rooms is to be kept confidential unless there is an agreement to disclose it to the other side. This way, the parties can be more open and honest with the mediator than if they were all in the same room.

In addition, when I mediate, I have reviewed the mediation summaries in advance. A good mediator will have a handle on the issues from the mediation summaries and should have some ideas going in as to what approach might make sense to settle the divorce. When I mediate, I tell everyone that there is no settlement of your divorce until every issue is resolved. Often, we make a list and work through the issues one by one, coming to tentative resolutions. I usually ask each party in private: What do you really want and why?

In some divorces, a mediation session of two or three hours can resolve the case. In other, more complicated divorces, or those where there is a lot of acrimony and emotion, it may take several sessions. I have had cases where there were seemingly insurmountable issues regarding substance abuse, infidelity, and gambling. But a good mediator can usually get the job done if you and your spouse are each willing to compromise. If you give in on one issue and your spouse is willing to give a little on another, a global settlement can be achieved.

Often when I am mediating, I make suggestions to spouses and their attorneys as to how to break a deadlock. I sometimes tell the parties in the separate rooms what I believe a judge may or not do with an issue – or the entire divorce – if it goes to trial. With this information during a phase when they still have control over their fates, as opposed to totally losing control by going to trial, most mediations result in a settlement.

Once a settlement is achieved, it's put in writing or recorded and becomes the basis for the divorce judgment and settlement agreement. There is no trial, and the parties simply go to court to end the divorce in a civil fashion. Mediation can save you thousands of dollars in costs and attorneys as well as the emotional toll that goes hand in hand with continuing to fight your divorce through the courts.

In marriages where there is a history of domestic violence, mediation may not work. Decisions must be carefully made as to whether to put an abused spouse into a mediation or arbitration situation where there may not be sufficient safeguards to protect the abuse victim. Domestic violence screening can be critical here.

ARBITRATION

When all else fails and you want some type of resolution of your divorce instead of going to trial, arbitration is the next option.

In arbitration, a written agreement or contract is drawn up and signed by the spouses and their attorneys. The parties agree to appoint a lawyer or retired judge who will hear the case in a more formal setting than mediation and rule on the issues in writing as a judge would after a trial.

Why not just go straight to trial instead? There are several reasons. Over the years, I have had cases that should have taken several hours end up taking several days in court. With arbitration, you set a time and day for the hearing. You then go to the office where the arbitration is to take place and get started. There are no interruptions and you go for as many hours as everyone agrees to.

On the other hand, when you go to court, there are always delays and interruptions. A day in court where you hope to have six or seven hours of trial time in actuality turns out to be two or three.

In court, there are usually several matters set at the same time. The judge will start the day at 8:30 or 9 a.m. and then go through a series of other cases, sometimes putting settled cases on the record, maybe discussing issues with parties, and setting trial dates. This all takes time, as do lunch and other breaks that routinely occur.

In many cases, judges take a few hours of testimony and then adjourn to another day. Held a few hours at a time, a trial can last for months.

Also, you can pick your arbitrator, but you can't pick your judge. I have had many wonderful judges over the years, but some who were not. I recall one case when the judge called the attorneys into his chambers before the trial was to start, pulled out a coin, and said, "Call it." I have known others who had biases or preconceived notions that influenced the way they interpreted the facts. Some judges have no business being a judge; they have little background in divorce and little stomach for the emotional overlay that comes with it.

As I have said repeatedly, once you go before a judge, you and your spouse are no longer making the decisions about your lives and those of your children; at that point, a stranger who doesn't know you and in some cases couldn't care less about you is deciding some of the most important issues concerning your family.

A trained expert in family law who is arbitrating your case can get to the nitty-gritty much faster then many judges can or will. And in arbitration, you can set your own rules. You can be as informal or formal as you like. You can set the rules regarding witnesses and the rules of evidence to fit your needs. This is not typical in a formal trial.

While hiring an arbitrator can be costly, the expenses are normally split between the spouses. In addition, arbitration can streamline the process; a divorce that might take a week or more in court could be done in half the time with a skilled arbitrator.

What are the possible disadvantages? First, if there is a history of domestic violence in your marriage, arbitration may not be right for you. You must be sure that there is full protection for you in the event of arbitration if you and/or your children have been victims of domestic violence in the marriage.

Second, if you are unhappy with the arbitrator's decision, it is much more difficult to appeal an arbitrator's award or ruling than it is to appeal that of a judge following trial.

I have been involved in many arbitration hearings — as an arbitrator and representing one of the parties to a divorce. Before you make a decision on going with arbitration, seek the advice and counsel of your attorney to determine whether arbitration is in your best interests. It is not an easy decision.

GOING TO TRIAL

Less than 1 percent of my divorce cases go to trial. With the winnowing out process that starts from the informality of a couple sitting down and working out their issues to the other extreme of arbitration, very few divorces are left to go to trial.

When divorces do go to trial, though, it's because some attorneys refuse to look at solutions or are unable to properly advise their clients. Also, for some cases — especially those with complicated custody or financial issues where no matter what is tried, an agreement cannot be reached — a trial becomes the last and only resort. A trial may also be the only solution in situations when there are emotional or mental problems on the part of one or both of the parties. When anger and bitterness are so great that you and your spouse can't let go and move on, refusing all other solutions and attempts at an agreement along the way, a trial may become inevitable.

That's unfortunate. Trials are emotionally draining for everyone involved — for the attorneys, for you and your soon-to-be former spouse, for your children to the extent that they are involved, and for any experts who are called to testify. I strongly believe that children should never appear in court. Where I practice, judges considering custody issues talk to children privately in chambers. They keep such discussions confidential to protect the children.

In some cases, the parties can agree to a summary trial. Let me explain how this works. I was involved in a high-conflict divorce where there was not a lot of money, but there was a lot of debt, and a formal trial would have taken several days. However, the parties could not agree on the time of day, much less who got what. We worked out an agreement, similar to a trial brief, with a written order to have a trial in which a written memorandum was submitted to the court in advance, outlining the history of the marriage, assets, liabilities, and all issues. It also included a request for relief. As part of this, we agreed to waive the rules of evidence and let each spouse present any evidence that he or she wanted to introduce with the understanding that everything would be reviewed by the judge before a decision was made.

We agreed to present no witnesses and only have the husband and wife each speak for an hour. There would be no direct or cross-examination, and there would be no interruptions. Each attorney would give a brief opening statement, and a short 15-minute closing following the clients' testimony. That was it. A trial that could have taken several days was reduced to less than one. This model allows both parties the opportunity to get what they want to say off their chest. However, it helps avoid the cost and acrimony of a regular trial, which can be formal – and expensive.

I have talked to many judges over the years and all agree that they would rather have the parties make their own decisions than be put in the position of having to rule. The judges don't know you, and they might not like you much either after you have had your day in court. You will likely be unhappy with the results. And once you testify about everything that is wrong with your husband or wife, you can never take the words back. What you say on the record in open court is public, and could cause great wounds that never heal. This is critical, especially if you have children you are trying to raise together.

If you go to trial, be prepared. Make sure that every issue is covered in advance. If you do end up testifying in court, be brief and to the point, and do not ramble. And by all means, do not lie in court. Fibbing on even a minor issue will destroy your credibility for everything else.

ABOUT ATTORNEYS

I have already mentioned the importance of being represented by the right attorney and that there are attorneys who are problem solvers and others who create problems. You do not want the latter.

Some attorneys are always in trial. There are several reasons for this. One is that they will churn a file to create huge and often unnecessary costs and fees. The clients are encouraged to be more emotional, and this scorched earth tactic hurts everyone. At the end of the divorce, the attorneys have made a lot of money and the clients are left with fewer assets, more bitterness, and unhappiness. This is a lose-lose situation. This is not what you want for your divorce.

There are also attorneys who try cases because they can't advise their clients on ways to settle. Some let their clients run the case no matter what. Others are afraid to make recommendations or give opinions. You do not want this type of attorney.

A good lawyer will give advice and help you evaluate all of your options as you go through the divorce process. This is critical. A good attorney will also step back and look at the big picture. You do not want to be represented by someone who just sees everything your way and helps lead you down the path to disaster. You want — and are paying for — sound legal advice. You need an advocate, but don't want a lawyer who just follows you without offering opinions and advice based on his or her expertise.

Also, a good attorney will try to take control of a case as early as possible. I recently handled a divorce involving a long-term marriage and substantial assets. There were also some serious mental health issues on the part of one of the spouses. Right after the divorce was filed, I contacted the other attorney and suggested that we start meeting regularly to deal with issues as they came up rather then rushing off to the courthouse. Too many attorneys will file motions and go to court rather than meeting first to see if issues can be resolved or at least narrowed — this is so important no matter how little or much money you have and what issues there may be regarding your children. Talk first and go to court as a last resort. I cannot emphasize that too strongly!

LAST WORD

I have tried many cases. I have had clients who would not listen to me, and would not compromise. I have seen those same clients cry after a judge took away their children. I have seen people get the worst result possible because they would not listen to my advice.

Having your day in court should be a last resort, for when all else fails. A divorce trial is too often a sign of failure — by you and by your attorneys.

Wrapping Up

It's important to understand and weigh all of your options as you navigate your divorce to its conclusion. The steps to finalization include direct negotiation, collaborative law, mediation, arbitration, and — last but not least — the actual trial.

Notes

Notes

CHAPTER TWENTY-ONE

Your Final Papers

Once you and your spouse have reached an agreement addressing all of the issues between you, you will receive final papers for your divorce. They're called different things depending on the state where you live – a judgment of divorce, a decree for dissolution, a divorce decree, or similar. Regardless of the name, they have one purpose – to end your marriage.

The final decree is normally not modifiable and is final with regard to property, and in some instances, spousal support/alimony if it is structured as nonmodifiable.

Child-related issues including custody, parenting time/visitation, and child support are always modifiable, depending upon changes in circumstances and the laws of the state where you live.

KEY CATEGORIES

The final papers include a paragraph that officially ends your marriage and grants you a decree or judgment of divorce. Also look for:

- A provision dealing with spousal support or alimony. Either you or your spouse is going to receive it, or there will be a statement that no alimony will be paid as part of your divorce settlement.
- Language setting child custody and parenting time/visitation arrangements if you have minor children.
- Paragraphs addressing child support, including the amounts and duration.
- Provisions for medical insurance and uninsured medical expenses for your children. There may also be a paragraph dealing with medical insurance coverage and payments for you and your soon-to-be former spouse.

DISPOSITION OF PROPERTY

The next major portion of the agreement will discuss property, both real estate and personal, and how it is to be divided and transferred.

Any business entities will also be dealt with as part of the divorce decree or settlement agreement.

The agreement will address the division of savings and investments, along with any pensions, 401(k)s, and IRAs and other deferred or retirement accounts. These are often transferred through provisions that are called Qualified Domestic Relations Orders. They will be separate from the actual divorce decree, but should be discussed in the decree as well.

Motor vehicles, boats, planes, toys, and collections, as well as how your furniture and furnishings are to be dealt with, will also be addressed, as well as the payment of credit cards and other obligations. Life insurance and whether there is to be coverage for child support, alimony, or other obligations should be specified.

Some divorces will also include provisions covering college education for the children, and what to do about pets.

There can also be provisions for a religious decree — for example, a "Get," or release from the marriage by the husband in Judaism, or a divorce decree provision from a sheik if you are Muslim. There might even be clauses for cooperation regarding a Catholic annulment, which must be handled through the church.

Normally there will be security and enforcement provisions to make sure that everything is being properly divided, along with clauses dealing with discovery protection in the event of fraud, and bankruptcy should your former spouse file for bankruptcy and try to leave you holding the bag, so to speak. There may be provisions for attorney fees, and restoration of a prior or maiden name for the wife.

There can be clauses calling for penalties if one of the parties fails to follow the terms of the divorce settlement. In fact, a well-drafted final document or judgment of divorce or decree should cover as many contingencies as possible. There is an old saying that the devil is in the details and that is true in a divorce, as in other types of agreements.

All of the points in the divorce decree should be thoroughly explained to you by your attorney. If you have questions, do not be bashful. These papers are extremely important and can affect the rest of your life.

However, any agreement is only as good as the people who sign it. If you and your soon-to-be former spouse live up to the agreement, there should be no problems going forward. Conversely, if you or your former spouse are hell-bent on looking for ways to circumvent the agreement, expect to be back in court.

COVER ALL BASES

The key in developing your divorce agreement or decree is to make sure that all issues are properly and fully covered. The goal is to have finality, but also protection going forward. I cannot urge you enough to make sure that you have a good attorney assisting you through the entire process, including the final steps of having everything properly drafted. That is critical.

Bear in mind that normally a court speaks through its written orders. Even if you are in court to finalize your divorce on a given day, it's not final until the judgment or decree is signed by your judge and entered with the court.

A final word: Do not rush into a new marriage. I have had many clients remarry within days of the final decree being entered. This can be a recipe for disaster.

Let the dust settle. Wait at least two or three years to remarry. A hasty marriage usually leads to another divorce. You have been going through a difficult and crazy time. Give yourself time to heal and rebuild.

Wrapping Up

The final papers nail down all of the key points of your divorce resolution. Proper drafting of your final papers is critical to making sure that you are fully protected. Having a good and experienced divorce attorney is so important to making sure that happens.

Notes

Notes

CONCLUSION

Divorce is an economic, emotional, and legal journey. I wrote this book to provide you with a guide – to explain many of the situations that you will encounter before and during a divorce. It is not meant to be all inclusive. Many issues differ from state to state.

I've offered a lot of generalizations, but that is deliberate. While one size definitely does not fit all in a divorce, nor should it, there are many common issues that most people share as they navigate the rapids of a divorce.

Divorces are terrifying. Too often the legal system is far from user-friendly. Courts can be confusing to lawyers, who are human – as are judges. My intent is to lift the veil of secrecy that so often covers too much of what occurs in a divorce.

Communication is critical. You have a right to know what is going on with your attorney. You have a right to know how courts work. You need to know what to expect. I never oversell a case. I try to be realistic. To have you as a client, too many attorneys will paint an unrealistic picture of what you can expect. Don't fall into that trap.

Speaking of traps, just as the Internet and social media play an increasing role in every aspect of our lives, they have a more prominent part in the process of divorce. Until they get into court, many people haven't thought about the ripple effect of one ill-placed photo on Facebook or risky text message. Technology is commonly an instrument of evidence in divorce now. This is cutting-edge and an area in which I have specialized – and for that reason, focused on in this book.

My ultimate goal is to open your eyes to the realities of what may or may not happen on your divorce journey. I hope that these chapters have been useful and that you will go forward with dignity, knowing what to expect, how to act, and how to be more realistic. My aim is to help you learn and grow as you go through this difficult process. I hope that I have succeeded.

APPENDIX A

Budget Planner Worksheet

A. Housing Expenses

1.	**Rent**	
2.	**Mortgage payment**	
3.	**Property taxes**	
4.	**Appliance and house service contracts**	
5.	**House repairs**	
6.	**Gardening expense**	
7.	**Exterminator**	
8.	**Fuel oil**	
9.	**Gas**	
10.	**Electric**	
11.	**Water**	
12.	**Sewer**	
13.	**Garbage collection**	
14.	**Telephone/mobile phone**	
15.	**Cable television/Internet**	
16.	**Homeowner's association**	
17.	**Tips to doormen, etc.**	
18.	**Snow removal**	
19.	**House insurance**	
20.	**Household help**	

B. Household Expenses

1.	**Food** (including meat, milk, etc.)	
2.	**Cleaning and household supplies**	
3.	**Laundry and dry cleaning**	
4.	**Clothing for self**	
5.	**Clothing for children**	
6.	**Clothing for spouse**	

C. Auto Expenses/Transportation

1.	**Gasoline/oil**	
2.	**Maintenance and repairs**	
3.	**Loan/payments**	
4.	**Registration**	
5.	**Insurance**	
6.	**Parking/tolls**	
7.	**Commuting costs**	
8.	**Taxi/bus service**	
9.	**Other**	

D. Health Care Expenses (not covered by insurance)

1.	**Doctors - self**	
2.	**Doctors - children**	
3.	**Doctors - spouse**	
4.	**Dentists - self**	
5.	**Dentists - children**	
6.	**Dentists - spouse**	
7.	**Hospital**	
8.	**Psychotherapy** (for whom?)	
9.	**Medicine** (drugs)	
10.	**Vitamins**	
11.	**Medical specialists**	
12.	**Orthodontia**	
13.	**Allergy expense**	
14.	**Optical - self**	
15.	**Optical - children**	
16.	**Optical - spouse**	
17.	**Other medical expenses**	

E. Child Care Expenses

1.	**Lunch money**	
2.	**Allowance**	
3.	**Babysitter**	
4.	**Child grooming**	
5.	**Summer camp**	
6.	**Religious education**	
7.	**Tutoring**	
8.	**Lessons** (music, dancing, etc.)	
9.	**Pet expense**	
10.	**Education expense** (school supplies, tuition, books)	
11.	**Sports, extracurricular activities**	

F. Business Expenses

1.	**Dues** (union, etc.)	
2.	**Subscriptions, books**	
3.	**Other unreimbursed expenses** (specify)	
	a.	
	b.	
	c.	
4.	**Retirement plan**	

G. Personal Expenses

1.	**Tobacco**	
2.	**Grooming**	
3.	**Cosmetics**	
4.	**Lunches out**	
5.	**Entertainment**	
6.	**Vacations**	
7.	**Club dues and expenses**	
8.	**Religious dues and contributions**	
9.	**Gifts**	
10.	**Hobbies**	
11.	**Sports expenses**	
12.	**Education**	
13.	**Books, magazines, music, etc.**	
14.	**Charitable contributions**	

H. Insurance

1.	**Life insurance**	
2.	**Health insurance**	
3.	**Accident insurance**	
4.	**Disability insurance**	
5.	**Other** (specify)	

I. Obligations

1.	**Alimony**	
2.	**Child support**	
3.	**Loans** (other than auto)	
4.	**Other** (specify)	
	a.	
	b.	
	c.	
	d.	
	e.	
	f.	

J. Recreation (not otherwise mentioned)

1.	**Other real estate**	
2.	**Boat expense**	
3.	**Airplane expense**	
4.	**Motor home**	
5.	**Motorcycle**	
6.	**Pets & equipment**	

G. Other Expenses

1.	**Federal income tax**	
2.	**State income tax**	
3.	**City/local income taxes**	
4.	**Social Security taxes**	
5.	**Medicare/Medicaid**	

Total Monthly Expenses	
Total Annual Expenses	

Notes

_____

_____

_____

_____

_____

_____

_____

_____

_____

_____

_____

_____

_____

_____

_____

_____

_____

_____

_____

_____

_____

_____

_____

Notes

Notes

_____

_____

_____

_____

_____

_____

_____

_____

_____

_____

_____

_____

_____

_____

_____

_____

_____

_____

_____

_____

_____

_____

_____

_____

_____

_____

INDEX

D

E

F

G

ABOUT THE AUTHOR

Attorney Henry S. Gornbein is a leading expert in family law. Practicing in Michigan for more than 40 years, he has written extensively on divorce-related topics.

Gornbein wrote the chapter, "Spousal Support," in the book, *Michigan Family Law*. It's the go-to source for all family law attorneys and judges who deal with divorce and related issues in Michigan. His articles appear regularly in national legal publications and his monthly column, "Case of the Issue," runs in the *Family Law Section Journal* of the State Bar of Michigan and is read by thousands of lawyers and judges.

A contributor and blogger for *The Huffington Post* Divorce section, he also produces regular podcasts for *divorcesourceradio.com*. In addition, Gornbein has hosted and produced his own Philo Award-winning cable TV show, *Practical Law*, with more than 700 programs aired to date.

Sought after as an expert on divorce-related topics by media outlets, he is known for being at the forefront of understanding social media and its role in divorces today. Recently, Gornbein has been speaking for a series of webinars discussing the impact of social media on divorce, along with issues including wiretapping, computer hacking, spycams, and others that can arise during divorce and have criminal law violation implications.

Other attorneys and judges consult Gornbein as an expert when unusual family law issues arise. A frequent public speaker for local and national meetings, he has been a featured lecturer at the National Convention of the American Academy of Matrimonial Lawyers.

Gornbein is married to Debra Gornbein, and is a father and grandfather. He is a named partner in the Birmingham, Michigan, law firm of Lippitt O'Keefe Gornbein, PLLC, where he heads the divorce and family law unit.

Gornbein enjoys travel, reading, theater, and movies, but most of all, spending time with his wife, children, and grandchildren.